"Men often struggle with talking abou
been conditioned to stuff their emotions. Jonathan
a bold, liberating, and refreshing book. Every pastor needs copies of
this book on the shelf to help men of all ages grieve well."

TED CUNNINGHAM
senior pastor, Woodland Hills Family Church, Branson, MO
author of *Young and in Love*

"As the director of M.E.N.D. (Mommies Enduring Neonatal Death),
I'm often asked if there are any good resources for the daddies. Until
now, there really wasn't a great book I could recommend to these
hurting men. Jonathan covers it all in *Grieve Like a Man*. He candidly
tells of his own numerous and varied losses and how he endured the
grief following each one. He provides personal application questions
to consider and concludes each chapter with reflection questions. This
book is not just for men. I recommend that women read it in order to
get a better understanding of how men are wired to deal with loss and
death. Anyone who has suffered some type of loss will greatly benefit
from reading this wonderful and well-written resource."

REBEKAH MITCHELL
founder and president, M.E.N.D.

"Grief can take men and women alike into a wilderness that's unfamiliar,
frightening, and potentially overwhelming. Many times, however, men
especially stumble through that wilderness in ways that compound
their pain. In *Grieve Like a Man*, Jonathan Fann speaks openly from
his and his wife Heather's own personal experience, as well as from
his ministry as a chaplain, in order to help men face and deal with
grief—for their own sake as well as for their loved ones. The "markers"
he describes draw upon Scripture and provide valuable insights for
navigating through this strange and terrible terrain. Bless yourself,
or someone you know who's walking through grief, with this book."

PRESTON PARRISH
author of *Finding Hope in Times of Grief*

Grieve
Like A Man

Jonathan Fann

HARVEST HOUSE PUBLISHERS

EUGENE, OREGON

Cover by Koechel Peterson & Associates, Inc., Minneapolis, Minnesota

Cover photo © Hemera/Thinkstock

GRIEVE LIKE A MAN
Copyright © 2012 by Jonathan Fann
Published by Harvest House Publishers
Eugene, Oregon 97402
www.harvesthousepublishers.com

Library of Congress Cataloging-in-Publication Data
    Fann, Jonathan, 1976-
    Grieve like a man / Jonathan Fann.
       p. cm.
    ISBN 978-0-7369-3925-6 (pbk.)
    ISBN 978-0-7369-4237-9 (eBook)
    1. Christian men—Religious life. 2. Grief—Religious aspects—Christianity. 3. Grief in men. I. Title.
    BV4528.2.F36 2012
    248.8'66—dc23

                                                  2011021675

Printed in the United States of America

12 13 14 15 16 17 18 / BP-NI / 10 9 8 7 6 5 4 3 2 1

To our children in heaven—
Caleb and August

ACKNOWLEDGMENTS

I learned the grief markers in this book because many loved ones made the decision to walk with me on my grief journey. My wife, Heather, was there throughout, and to her I offer my greatest thanks. She showed patience and unconditional love even as I was learning what it meant to grieve like a man. I couldn't have asked for a better partner in grief or in life, and this book wouldn't exist without her. Countless friends and family members found themselves tossed into this journey with us, and I thank all of them for their love, support, and compassion.

To Peter, Kasie, Luke, Mikayla, David, Allison, Jason, Amy, Ray, and Leah, I also say thank you. As a group you allowed Heather and me to hurt without ever trying to fix us. God placed you in our lives in a very difficult season, and I am so grateful He did. David, thank you for taking time out of your busy schedule to review this manuscript and offer valuable suggestions.

I am grateful to Rebekah, who chose amid the grief of losing her son Jonathan to create a support group for other hurting parents. Mommies Enduring Neonatal Death (M.E.N.D.) gave us a place to voice our hurt and to find encouragement from others who survived similar losses.

My friends Randy and Kathryn believed in this project when it was just an idea I discussed at dinner. Kathryn, thank you for the excitement and motivation that got this book started well. Phil and Jennifer, you both have taught me so much, and I thank you for your inspiration and wisdom.

I would also like to thank the men who trusted me to share their stories of loss in this book. Each one was open and authentic, hoping that his story might help others.

Sara Elliott spent countless hours with this manuscript in its various forms. It is a better work because it passed through her hands. Thank you, Sara, for using your time and talents so generously to help others. Thank you even more for the friendship and love you continue to show Heather and me.

Contents

Foreword

WHEN GOD CREATED THE GARDEN OF EDEN, He made no provision for death within its lush surroundings. Eden had no hospice and no cemetery.

The fact is, we weren't created to die. Alzheimer's, heart attacks, miscarriage, cancer, and fatal accidents would have been misfits in the garden.

Death was an intruder in Eden.

When people we love die, it will always feel counterintuitive because it's counter-creation. God created us to be uncorrupted by sin, untouched by death. But when sin entered the garden, death entered our race.

Death—and something else.

Grief.

Grief is a strange thing. It shows up uninvited, comes for all sorts of reasons, and stays longer than we ever expect. No one knows quite how to grieve, but we all have to at some point. Jonathan Fann never expected to have to deal with the fatigue, despair, and frustration that grief brought him. Before he was 30 years old, he had lost his law-enforcement career due to an injury; his firstborn son, Caleb, who lived only six hours; his second child, August, who miscarried; and his father, who died suddenly at age 57.

Job said, "My face is flushed from weeping, and deep darkness is on my eyelids...my days are passed, my plans are torn apart, even the wishes of my heart" (Job 16:16; 17:11 NASB). Jon had to have felt the same way. But unlike Job, he didn't sprinkle his head with ashes and clothe himself in sackcloth. Instead, he kept working, tried to console his wife, stayed busy, and slowly imploded. Grief doesn't leave just because it is ignored. Instead, it lodges in places where it eventually will be acknowledged. That's what happened to Jon. His path brought him to the hard reality that men grieve...they just may grieve differently than the women they love.

In Scripture, we're told to "mourn with those who mourn" or to "grieve with those who grieve" (Romans 12:15). Paul didn't tell us to analyze those who grieve. He didn't tell us to fix or scold those who are struggling after loss or change. He didn't suggest we give a to-do list to those who mourn so they can snap out of it faster. Perhaps that's because the biggest need people have when they grieve is the assurance that they aren't alone—that someone understands. When we grieve, we simply need someone to walk with us and feel what we're feeling.

You may have picked up this book because you intuitively

knew you needed a knowing voice to speak into your grief. Friend, you have chosen wisely. Man to man, friend to friend, Jonathan will walk with you and honestly share what worked for him during his season of grief.

Men can't fix grief. They simply have to feel it and deal with it in the way they are wired. *Grieve Like a Man* gives men permission to do just that. It also gives women an insider's view of how men grieve when they experience loss.

As you take this book into your hands, let it seep into your heart. Trust it. Trust the truth that will comfort you. Trust the wisdom that will bring clarity and empathy to you. God can use grief to deepen and strengthen you.

You may grieve loss and wipe away tears of remembrance— tears that confirm that Eden had no tombstones. Ultimately, may your mourning contain glimmers of hope that remind you that life, not death, is our ultimate reality.

But, in the meantime, we may grieve. So free yourself to do so…like a man.

Dr. Philip and Jennifer Rothschild
cofounders of Womensministry.net
and Fresh Grounded Faith Events

Jennifer is the author of
Lessons I Learned in the Dark
and *Self Talk, Soul Talk*

Introduction

I WAS IN THE MIDDLE OF WORKING THIRD SHIFT. Most cops will tell you it can get pretty boring after three a.m. The bars have all closed, and most of the troublemakers have gone home. This is usually a good time to catch up on reports from earlier in the night or to finally check on some of the low-priority complaints.

This particular night had been unusually quiet, so I was getting bored. I jumped at the opportunity to provide backup for an officer in the next beat. He was checking on a complaint about someone selling drugs out of a house. It was a routine call, but at least it was something to do. I spent most of the drive thinking about where to take a break after the call was over.

The house was in a rough part of the city, an area known for drugs and many other unsavory things. As I approached, I could see the glow of a television through one of the windows. I met up with my partner for the call, and we walked to the door. When he knocked, I watched a woman walk across the room to answer. When she opened the door, my partner explained that someone called and said drugs were being sold out of her home. Of course, the woman denied the accusation and invited us to search the house.

Most people who make an invitation like this are trying to prove there aren't any drugs in the house. That's a rookie mistake. For some reason, drug dealers always think they're smarter than the cops and have the only foolproof hiding spot imaginable. In fact, drug paraphernalia was clearly visible in the living room from the doorway. We secured the woman and did a quick check to see if anyone else was at the residence. We found one man in a back bedroom, and he wasn't very happy to see us. My partner entered the room first and immediately secured a loaded rifle that was propped in the corner. I asked the man to join us in the living area, and that's when it happened.

If you've ever been in a traffic accident, you know the strange sensation of life going into slow motion. A split second seems to last for an entire minute. This is exactly what happened to me as this man reached for a gun. He was sitting on a mattress on the floor, and next to the mattress was a black handgun. When I saw the gun, I quickly drew my duty weapon. I yelled a warning—"No!"

He continued to reach for the gun.

I yelled again, "No!" I knew from my training that as soon as he touched the gun I had to fire or risk him getting off a shot. The adrenaline was kicking in, making me hyper-focused. His hand was now an inch above the gun. My .40 caliber Glock was trained directly on his chest. I moved my finger to the trigger and began to squeeze. I would fire twice and then evaluate, just as I was trained. I screamed, "No!" for the last time.

Suddenly, the man pulled his hand back. I removed my finger from the trigger as my partner moved to secure the handgun and the suspect. Less than an inch separated this man from changing both of our lives forever.

My partner then searched the house while I guarded the two suspects. I looked at my hands—they were shaking in an attempt to get rid of the remaining adrenaline. We found the drugs and arrested the suspects.

As I worked through the remaining morning hours, I reflected on my actions. You can never be too sure how you'll react when a situation goes downhill and the intensity mounts. My partner and I were both safe, so I was pleased with my actions. I was doubly pleased that the suspect chose not to grab the gun.

I was 22 years old when this incident took place. I enjoyed my job—every day included something different, and I didn't have to sit in an office all day. The level of responsibility suited my personality well. I've always been a people person. At that point in my life, I couldn't imagine doing anything other than serving as a policeman. What more could a young man ask for? There were times of danger, excitement, and driving fast with sirens blaring. Admittedly, the job also included a lot of boredom, endless paperwork, and standing in the cold rain. It wasn't necessarily the perfect job, but I planned to see it through to retirement. But as is often the case, my plans didn't work out the way I expected.

About a year later I suffered a career-ending injury. There isn't even an exciting story to tell—it was simply a training accident. It left me with a destroyed knee. After two surgeries, each followed by six months of rehab, the verdict came in: My days as a cop were over.

Initially, I thought this was just another exciting adventure in my life, and I looked forward to seeing what would happen next. That initial optimism faded when reality began to set in. I had become a cop through and through. All my friends were cops, and everything I did outside of work either involved family or other cops. A special camaraderie exists when you entrust your life to the people you work with. My identity had become wrapped up in my job.

As time passed, I continued to spend time with those same people, but eventually we had less and less in common. I was able to hold my own for a while with old war stories, but even I grew sick of hearing them repeated. I became less connected with the life of a cop, and as a result, I became depressed.

In hindsight, it's clear that I was in a perfect storm of grief and had no clue how to deal with it. I had lost my job, my friends, my physical abilities, and my identity. I no longer had an answer for that all-too-common question, "What do you do?" My self-esteem was at an all-time low. After all, wasn't it just the other day that I was responsible for life-and-death decisions?

In my depression, I failed to recognize my need to grieve my losses. As a result, my grief began manifesting itself in other ways. I became angry all the time, and I didn't know why. In the absence of many friends, my wife was left to deal with my moodiness. It was a strain on our marriage. I had also begun to believe the lies I was telling myself. I thought I was worthless and didn't have anything left to contribute to the world. I became lethargic and lazy.

I took years to learn that I needed to grieve. When I chose

to recognize that need and deal with it, I was finally able to move forward. I can't help but wonder, though, how much pain could have been avoided if I'd understood my grief sooner. For that reason, I hope this book will provide that early understanding for you—insight into your grief that will keep you from making mistakes that cause needless pain.

Everyone's situation is different. What has happened to you is different from what happened to me. You may be reading this after losing a job or closing the door on your failed business. Your wife may have just walked out the door, vowing never to return. You may have just buried a child, spouse, sibling, parent, or friend. You may still be reeling after learning that a lifelong dream will never come true. Perhaps you're caught in the continual and complicated grief that comes from watching a loved one battle Alzheimer's or some other tragic disease. Whatever your loss, I want you to know that there *is* hope, and you can realize that hope by choosing to accept your grief and start the process of healing.

In addition to having a unique situation, each man has a unique way of grieving. You will not grieve your losses the same way I grieve mine. My goal in this book is for us to learn from our shared experience so you can apply what you learn to your own particular grief, your personality, and your comfort level.

Grief is a journey we must all take at some point in our lives. I compare this journey to a hiking trail. Parts of this trail are well-worn by the many travelers who went before us, but other sections require us to choose our own way through paths we've never walked before. Thankfully, our trail has some markers and signposts along the way. Those markers provide valuable information that is either immediately relevant or useful at some later point on the trail. Some markers may not apply to your situation, but as you travel the path of grief, if you fail to see any markers, you might have gotten off the trail or even wandered into a danger zone.

What follows isn't a how-to manual or a step-by-step process. It's a series of markers to serve as guides and warnings. Apply the markers that are relevant to your unique situation and that will aid you on your grief journey. This will help you avoid two common mistakes men make as part of their grief—either they deny it altogether or they try to adopt the grief markers that are intended for women.

Denial is a tactic many of us learned as young boys. Someone probably told us something like this: "Just be strong. Boys don't cry." Most men eventually recognize that this tough-guy attitude toward grief just doesn't work. Maybe that realization is what prompted you to pick up this book. As a cop, I became a master at this macho persona, and it most definitely did not serve me well.

So what happens when you finally become convinced that simply gritting your teeth and plowing forward will not work?

Without a guide or markers specific to men, many men grieve the only way they know how—the way they've seen women do it. As a chaplain for a hospice, in a hospital, and in the Army, I have seen this cause problems in many relationships. There are certainly similarities between the way men and women grieve, but there are also many God-given differences.

The wives, mothers, sisters, and female friends who are called into a grief journey with the men in their lives will also learn valuable insights from the markers we'll consider in the following pages. They will learn to recognize some of the different characteristics of men's grief. This knowledge can provide reassurance that the men they love are indeed grieving even when that grief looks very different from their own.

The goal is for the grieving man to acknowledge and work through his grief and come out the other side. Often, the man who emerges from his grief is different than he was before. He comes out stronger.

As for me, I moved on with my new life. After I grieved the losses associated with being a cop, I began the slow transition to becoming a chaplain. During that time I entered another incredibly painful season of grief. The losses awaiting me were more difficult than anything I could have imagined. Many of the markers were brought to my attention by others who helped me through that time. Some of the markers became obvious as I progressed through my grief, but I didn't notice others until later as I reflected back on my experience. I am convinced that men should never again have to settle for simply burying their grief or processing it in unhelpful ways. There is another choice, and it is my hope that the eleven markers that follow will be faithful signposts for your journey.

1

I Don't Have Time for This

Grief is never convenient.

LIFE WAS GREAT! Heather and I were living out fantastic days together. Our marriage was stronger than ever, and we stood ready for a new adventure. I had worked through my grief and was finally able to put my life as a cop behind me. Next up—the ministry!

We were going to put everything on the line for our new life. So with that wonderful mixture of excitement and terror that comes with risking everything for the unknown, we packed our bags and moved to Dallas for graduate school.

We were a little worried about what it would be like to live in such a large city so far away from family and friends. We also had all the usual concerns related to going back to school—I had not been the most dedicated student in the past, and the idea of wasting tuition dollars made my stomach hurt. My wife depended on me, and we were about to have another mouth to feed. Heather was expecting our first child during this transition.

To say my faith was being stretched would be an understatement. I was stressed, but I also had an incredible peace. In fact, it was one of the happiest times in my life. I knew God had set me on this journey. It was an exciting feeling to rely on Him in such a real way from day to day. I had no other choice. Questions hung heavy, of course, and I certainly didn't have the answers. I remember praying, *God, I have no idea how this is going to work out, so I just trust it to You.* I must have said that a thousand times. God gave a thousand answers.

We settled in a small apartment just outside of Dallas. We managed to have enough money for my program so Heather—who had always dreamed of being a stay-at-home mom—was able to work at home.

I spent my days in class listening to debates, and then over dinner, Heather and I discussed what I had learned. One evening I was sitting at our dinner table while Heather finished cooking, and I breathed a silent prayer. *God, You are so good to me. Life is so perfect right now, and I thank You for bringing me here.*

The anxieties associated with our move had begun to fade. We had a nice apartment, and I quickly learned the new driving skills I needed to commute to downtown Dallas. God even threw in a huge park close to home so I could enjoy short escapes from all the sirens and car alarms in our neighborhood.

The only unknown for me had to do with being a dad. Like most new fathers, I wondered if I had what it takes. Would I really be able to live up to that dangerous comment I had made numerous times—"My kids will never act like that!"

It's a Boy

Soon our small nursery was ready for its new occupant, and so was I. As I walked past the nursery doorway, my mind drifted to thoughts of my soon-to-arrive son. A boy. Heather wouldn't let me register for baby gifts at Bass Pro Shops or Cabela's, but the day was coming when he would be all Dad's. It is amazing how your mind can drift instantly to the dreams you have for your son—even one you haven't met. Hunting is a big deal for the men in my family, so it was no surprise that my thoughts drifted to the first year he would join the rest of the men at deer camp.

A few years after that I would allow him to select a special hunting knife. I could almost see myself teaching him how to field dress and skin a deer with that very knife. As my thoughts continued to race outside that nursery door, I imagined him finally getting to carry a rifle and take a deer for himself. These daydreams were based on my own childhood because those were exactly the same steps I took with my dad. They would be his unforgettable rites of passage, and I would be there to guide him every step of the way. With every dream I grew more excited for my son's arrival.

About halfway through my first semester, we experienced a big challenge. On November 1, Heather entered the hospital for bed rest because of complications with the pregnancy. Our son wasn't due to arrive for almost three months, so this was a serious matter. Even so, I remained calm. I was focused on

God, and I felt that part of the reason He brought us to Dallas was so we could benefit from Baylor University Medical Center and all its resources and expertise.

Heather stayed as busy as possible while confined to a hospital bed. She was blessed with several visits from our mothers. They kept watch while I tried to stay on pace in school. I wrote papers and read theology at her bedside and in the hospital lounge. It was a time of uncertainty, but it also included some good memories. Heather and I both really enjoyed watching football, and her room had all the sports channels. I decided to provide the snacks for some of these sporting events to give Heather a break from hospital food and also to justify my junk-food craving. Heather used discretion and fared well after these bedside picnics, but I learned there are just some things you do not mix with fake crab meat.

We developed some wonderful friendships with Heather's nurses. Two in particular, Kelly and Teresa, still hold special places in our hearts. They spoiled Heather and gave us both a lot of leeway as we yelled at the television during the games.

The doctor was hoping to let our son grow as long as possible before being born, but on December 1, the baby showed signs of distress. I got a call at the apartment early that morning to return to the hospital. I called family and friends to share the wonderful news that our son would arrive later that day. Two carloads of family began the seven-hour drive to Dallas. Later that morning, the doctors decided it was best not to wait any longer, so our son, Caleb Scott, was born at 11:12 a.m. and taken to the neonatal intensive care unit (NICU). This was all according to plan and something we expected. I made all the calls to announce our little blessing had arrived.

I assumed all would be well now that Caleb was here. But later that day, Heather and I met with a doctor who explained Caleb was much sicker than we had anticipated. I still had peace though, and I made another round of calls asking for prayer. I just knew God was going to heal my son for His glory. How could God not answer this prayer? After all, He had come through in so many other areas.

Only a few hours later, the nurses took us to the NICU with little explanation, and we knew something wasn't right. Several nurses and a doctor surrounded Caleb's tiny bed. They were talking and moving quickly. Then suddenly, the room went quiet. No one was talking, and the machines grew silent. Through tears we watched helplessly as our Caleb died. His entire life had been just a little more than six hours. The nurses cleaned his tiny body and put him in a yellow outfit. The nurse who handed Caleb to Heather was crying as hard as we were. We held our son close, ran our fingers over his tiny features, kissed him, and said goodbye. Then we returned to Heather's room, held each other, and cried.

Devastation

The pendulum that had been our wonderful life now began to swing the other way as we descended toward devastation. In the days ahead I would quickly learn two things: Grief never comes at a convenient time, and this leaves us men with a choice. When a life-shattering loss occurs, we can do what is good, or we can do what is great.

Though I was still in shock and pain, a hundred things seemed to demand my attention at once. I didn't have the luxury of waiting for a more convenient time.

First, with God's help, I chose to focus on the great thing that needed to be done. I poured my attention and energy into taking care of and protecting my wife. This is one of the keys to recognizing the great over the good—the great has to do with people, whereas the good consists mainly of tasks. Naturally, at such times, tasks can seem urgent, and they do offer opportunities to stay busy and fix things. Most of us men have a built-in desire to fix problems, but hurting people are not quickly or easily fixed.

One reason that people represent the greater choice is that they draw out your personal greatness. You enter into situations that force you to draw on One greater than yourself.

Whatever your loss may be, there are likely others who need your help during the crisis. Often, that just means being there to the fullest. Leave your cell phone in the car and choose to give your best to the hurting person. Decisions that need to be made at your job can be made by someone else. Projects that must be completed can be finished by someone else. Most of us believe we are irreplaceable at work. We're not. But we *are* irreplaceable when it comes to offering other people what they need in those early days of grief.

The Temptation of the Good

The good has a further temptation—it's usually much easier than the great. For instance, when some men face a personal tragedy, they look to their work as a seemingly valid excuse to avoid grief, especially in those first few days. By working hard and avoiding your pain, you may even get some praise from your boss, who will express his admiration for your devotion to your job during a difficult time. But actually, this choice will only complicate your grief in the long run.

I can recall a man who chose to miss a family member's funeral because of work. He sent the rest of his family to the out-of-town service and has regretted it ever since. He was left not only with the grief surrounding the loss of someone he cared about deeply but also with the grief that accompanies a poor decision.

Our losses are tough enough without adding regrets. If you've made such a choice, admit it and move on. You may need to make an apology, or you may simply need to forgive yourself. We all make mistakes, and you can choose to walk past this one on your journey.

In those first days after Caleb's death, I could have easily transitioned my wife's care to other family members as they arrived. I had all the excuses in the world to stay busy elsewhere; after all, thousands of dollars in tuition and tens of thousands of dollars in hospital bills were on the line.

I could have focused on these issues and ignored Heather, justifying my actions with the excuse that this too was a way of taking care of my family. To be honest, that choice would have been easier. I knew what calls to make and what offices to visit, but I had no idea how to help my wife or how to deal with what was going on inside of me. I felt overwhelmed. Still, somehow I knew that I belonged at Heather's side.

After we cried together for some time, I started to make the last round of phone calls to family and friends. There were still two carloads of family on the way, and they needed some time to process the news before they arrived at the hospital. I'm glad I did this instead of allowing someone else to make the calls, but it was hard.

I was shaken when I spoke to my dad on the phone. My mom was in one of the carloads on the way to the hospital, so he was alone at home. He wept uncontrollably. I don't ever remember my father crying before this. Choosing to make this call instead of focusing on another distraction ripped me to the core, but the relational connection with my dad was worth the pain. It was the first time since I was a young child that I could remember my dad and I saying "I love you" to each other. It was a good memory from a tragic day.

The Distraction of the Good

Years have passed since those difficult days. I graduated from seminary and accepted a position as a hospice chaplain, where I had the honor of walking with many men through their initial days of grief. These men knew their loved ones—often their wives—were approaching death. I have observed recurring patterns in these men after their wives died. Most spent a while at the bedside. I am sometimes invited to join them in these precious moments. I will pray and offer to read Scripture. The men will usually talk to their wives, touch them, and say goodbye.

As we leave the room together, their minds will almost always turn to the distraction of the good. They ask questions about moving the loved one's belongings out of the long-term care facility, how to get a death certificate, and who will call the funeral home. These are all good questions, and I answer each one carefully while assuring the widowers that everything is in place to address those details. For some, this gives them permission to focus on the greater matters at hand. They can call family, friends, and pastors to join them in their grief. Others, however, find comfort in the distractions. After their questions are answered, they simply find something else to hold their focus. In the needless busyness, they seek some level of control in a world that has just spiraled out of control.

My ministry includes following up on these men after the deaths of their loved ones. I consistently see a difference between the men who accepted their grief and the men who focused on the distractions at hand. Those who waited for a more convenient time to grieve usually realized later that they missed some great blessings by not facing their grief head-on at the outset. By the time they realize this, their families may have all returned home. The words, hugs, and support were all initially there, but the distracted widower did not fully feel their impact. I gently offer these men the same advice I offer you: *Now* is the time to begin the grief journey.

The Foot of the Cross

One man's grief journey took him to a most unlikely place as he faced the choice of completing good tasks or rising to the greater challenge of focusing on relationships. John, one of Jesus' twelve disciples, made his decision at the foot of Jesus' cross. To fully grasp the storm of grief that had enveloped John, we need to know a little more about him. John was one of the twelve disciples, but his relationship with Jesus went deeper than that. He was one of three disciples who often received special training and revelation from Jesus. John highlights his affection for Jesus when he tells us that he was known as "the disciple whom Jesus loved."

John was convinced that Jesus was the Messiah and was

on the verge of ushering in His kingdom. John had been with Jesus for about three years and by then was no doubt anticipating a leadership role of his own in the new kingdom.

John was with Jesus the night He was betrayed and arrested. As the night continued into the next day, Jesus was mocked, tortured, and interrogated in a series of illegal trials. John's grief must have multiplied as questions filled his mind. *Why is this happening? Why won't Jesus stop it? Jesus is the Messiah we were waiting for, isn't He? Surely they won't kill Him, will they? Will they come after us next?*

Many of us men can imagine John's anguish because we too have spent sleepless nights with our minds flooded by a torrent of questions. The answers never come easy amid the hazy thinking of early grief.

As the narrative of Jesus' crucifixion advanced, John's losses must have seemed to be multiplying. First he lost a friend named Judas, the disciple who betrayed Jesus. They had been together for three years, and John's heart must have broken as he watched Judas lead the armed crowd straight to Jesus.

In one of the most gut-wrenching scenes I've ever witnessed, a pastor removed an elder—one of his best friends—from church leadership. Through tears, the pastor wept as he read a written statement concerning the elder's failure. He had to physically hold the podium to keep from collapsing about halfway through because the pain was so intense. Surely Judas' failure broke John's heart too.

Next, John lost his dreams, his career, and his hopes for the future. Jesus is being crucified, and that means John won't have a position in a new kingdom—a position he has spent the past three years training for and dreaming about. In his grief, John must have wondered, *What will I do now?* His identity was wrapped up in following Jesus, and the loss of an identity is terribly painful, especially for men.

Finally, in his clearest and most painful loss, John lost his friend and king, Jesus. Perhaps you have said goodbye to your closest friend and know all too well how John must have felt. Combine that pain with John's other losses, and his reaction is astounding. He doesn't run away, he doesn't isolate himself—he goes to the foot of the cross.

To fully appreciate the magnitude of John's decision, remember that this scene did not resemble our modern-day stained-glass windows or paintings of the event. This scene was more like a horror movie with the sights, sounds, and smells to match. John would have seen three crosses with Jesus hanging on the center one. His friend's body was stripped, mangled, and covered in blood. Roman soldiers keeping a close watch nearby must have glared at John with disdain. John would have heard the sound of the three crucified men gasping for air and groaning in pain. The unmistakable smell of death would have penetrated everything around it. It would have hung heavy in the air from previous executions. In the middle of this nightmare, racked with grief, John made two great choices.

"Standing by the cross of Jesus were His mother, His mother's sister, Mary the wife of Clopas, and Mary Magdalene" (John 19:25). In John's first opportunity to choose the great—to focus on his relationships with others—he took several women who were all followers of Jesus to the foot of the cross to say goodbye. One of those women was Mary, Jesus' own mother. What an amazing act of compassion. What might it have looked like, though, if John had chosen the good, focusing on tasks and trying to control the situation? He would have probably explained to these women that they couldn't go to the cross because the soldiers there might harm or even kill Jesus' followers. Jesus had loved them very much, so surely He wouldn't want them to take such a risk. John might have further explained to Mary that Jesus had been badly beaten and that she would not want that image as her last mental picture of Him. These suggestions would have been reasonable and based on genuine love, but John chose instead to be with those women and fulfill their needs.

"When Jesus saw His mother and the disciple He loved standing there, He said to His mother, 'Woman, here is your son.' Then He said to the disciple, 'Here is your mother.' And from that hour the disciple took her into his home" (verses 26-27). I must confess that I had read this passage numerous times, and my only thought was what an honor it must have been for John to take care of Jesus' mother, Mary. I failed to recognize the swamp of grief and related emotions John was dealing with when Jesus gave him this responsibility. John made another great choice amid his losses and chose to take care of Mary as if she were his own mother. He didn't even skip a beat, but took her into his home immediately.

What might have happened if John had kept his mind on the tasks at hand? He would have probably told Jesus that he was happy to help Mary. John would personally escort her to the house of one of Jesus' brothers; after all, they were the logical and legal choices to provide for Mary. John might have even explained that this choice made more sense because he was now unemployed with no current prospects for the future. You may laugh at the idea of John saying these things to Jesus, but isn't this exactly the way we sometimes initially react to grief—grasping for the things we can control and trying to fix at least something?

The beginning of grief will almost always prove inconvenient.

But at that critical time, *choose* to place your focus on people and the great things that being with them will do for your grief. Ask God to help you see the difference between good things and great things as you wrestle with the initial shock and numbness.

Perhaps your grief will reveal mistakes you have made. If so, I encourage you not to allow them to become insurmountable obstacles on your journey. Move past them by using what you have learned to help others and yourself. You will be reminded throughout this book that you can veer off the trail anytime, but the only way you remain lost is by refusing to return to the correct course.

Reflection Questions

1. What has distracted you from connecting with people in your early days of grief?

2. Are you still staying busy doing good things when greater things need your attention?

3. Do you need to forgive yourself for making poor decisions in those early days of grief?

4. Are you still waiting for a more convenient time to grieve?

2

I'm Drowning, but I Don't Need Help

Accepting help is not a sign of weakness.

WHEN I WAS YOUNG, I spent a day at a local water park with some of my friends. It was a large park, and our goal was to get on each ride at least once. We were all watching each other, so the crashes and splashes became more dramatic as we did our best to look cool.

On one particular ride, I was toward the end of the group, so I knew most of my buddies would be watching me from the bottom. It was a large, winding slide, and I was riding a tube down it. I decided to flip my tube as I reached the bottom for a little dramatic flair. I'm sure it looked cool, but I was unprepared for what happened next. At the base of the slide, the tubes carried riders into the middle of the pool. I no longer had a tube, so I was stuck at the bottom of the slide with other friends headed my way. Having another tube land on my head would definitely not look cool. There was a more serious problem than that, though. At the base of the slide, there was an extreme undertow from the water being pulled back to the top. I was a good swimmer, but the best I could do was simply maintain my distance from the slide. I wasn't able to swim away from it.

The watchful lifeguard reached his long pole in front of me to help me past the undertow. I can hardly put into words how much I did not want to grab that pole. My buddies were watching at the bottom, as were a couple of people who had just missed my head with their tubes. I would never hear the end of being saved by the lifeguard. Somehow I thought drowning would be more respectable. Eventually I came to my senses and grabbed the pole, and the lifeguard pulled me to safety. The only damage from the incident was to my pride.

The idea that my pride would cause me to reject a much-needed offer for help may seem absurd, but this is often exactly what men do when it comes to grief. At some point in their lives, many men buy the lie that to accept help is a sign of weakness.

In reality, asking others for help is often the smartest thing we can do. As you grieve, you may find that people are watching you, concerned about how you're doing. You may even feel like a goldfish from time to time. This feeling that everyone is watching may tempt you to act as if everything is fine and no help is required.

Stop and think in such a moment. Would your friends and family respect you more if you chose to drown or if you decided to accept the help God has provided? In your grief, you may feel powerless. I know I certainly did. Allowing others to help was like admitting there was one more thing in my life I couldn't control. I didn't know if my pride could take it. I was finally able to recognize that such help is a gift from God. In hindsight, I can see that accepting help while grieving is a lot like grabbing a lifeguard's pole. It may very well have saved my life.

Accepting Help

One of the great sources of help God sent us during the loss of Caleb was our family. In that first week after his death, family members surrounded us, and I found I appreciated their help. In the shock and numbness of our tragedy, I had made the great choice to focus on my wife and on my grief. That choice meant I needed other people to pick up the slack. One of the top priorities was to plan a funeral for Caleb. There were seemingly hundreds of details. My brother's wife, Jaime, and Heather's sister, Nikki, got busy. They knew that Caleb would need an outfit to be buried in. They asked me if they could shop for an outfit and bring a couple of choices for Heather to look at in the hospital while she was still recuperating. I hadn't even thought about a burial outfit, but those whom God gave us during this crisis knew what we needed.

God often provides help we don't even know we need. I could have told Jaime and Nikki that I would shop for the outfit myself, but that would have been my pride talking. Instead, they found two beautiful outfits. Heather and I chose one to be Caleb's burial gown. Insisting on doing the shopping myself would have been a twofold mistake. I wouldn't have been where I was needed the most, and Jaime and Nikki wouldn't have had the blessing of performing this act of love for Caleb. Remember that when you accept help, the person offering the help sometimes needs to do it just as much as you need to accept it.

Our parents offered to plan and pay for the funeral. Heather and I made the major decisions—we chose the songs, the items we wanted displayed at the front, and the day to have the service and visitation—but our families handled the details. They put our choices into action. Through our families' graciousness, they empowered us to make decisions without the hassle of making phone calls. As a result, we could spend more time making those major decisions. This was very important for us because some of those choices would be the only ones we would ever make for Caleb. Accepting the help of our loved ones not only gave me time for my grief but also allowed me to make better decisions.

Help also came in some of the more expected forms as well. We traveled back to Missouri so Caleb could be buried next to my grandparents. People brought more food to our families' homes than we could ever eat. Countless friends and loved ones attended the visitation and the funeral. As you would expect, they all offered to help in any way we needed.

Around this time, many people sent money instead of flowers or in addition to them. I love to give, but receiving is a different matter. My pride was getting in the way once again, and I felt bad for accepting the money. But later I realized that these gifts were very thoughtful. We used the money to treat ourselves on especially difficult days. Heather didn't have to cook, and we could grieve together while enjoying a meal out. It provided an excuse to simply get out of our apartment in those early weeks of grief, and that was very helpful.

The grieving men I minister to now as a hospice chaplain often have some unique needs. Many of them tell me they are from a generation of men who did everything themselves, and they don't want any help. Ironically, many of these same men spent their entire lives helping others through difficult times, but now that it's their turn to receive, they allow their pride to get in the way. This can lead to many grief complications, including isolation.

Many times after the loss of a spouse or an adult child, an older man will be unable to leave his house without assistance. He no longer sees friends or family, and the loneliness that he had already struggled with becomes seemingly insurmountable. The first thing I do to help such men is not to convince them that help is available, but to convince them that accepting help is not a sign of weakness. Those who accept the help are happier for various reasons and are able to progress on their grief journey. Pride, on the other hand, often causes the others to wander into some dangerous territory.

Asking for Help

In addition to accepting help when it's offered, you may find yourself having to ask for help even before it's offered. This is exactly where I found myself a couple of months after Caleb died. Fortunately, I had learned the value of accepting help, and that helped me to ask for it later on.

Heather had done some research and found a support group that dealt with our specific situation. It was within driving distance, and she wanted me to attend with her. I can't put into words just how much I didn't want to do this. I absolutely hated the idea. I had all kinds of false images about what I was getting myself into. In my mind I thought we would all have to hold hands, cry, and sing songs. I was also certain I would be the only man there. I'm glad I kept these concerns to myself. I knew Heather needed this group, so I agreed to attend a couple of times so she could meet some people and be comfortable going by herself.

At our first meeting, I was relieved to see that there were other men at the meeting after all. We sat in a circle of chairs and began by introducing ourselves and recounting the circumstances surrounding the deaths of our children. For some, it had been many years since their loss, but others were like us, having lost a child just a short time ago. When it was our turn, Heather introduced us to the rest of the group. I don't think I said anything at that first meeting. I simply listened. No one was forced to say anything; we could even pass on the introduction if we wished. I liked the format of sharing at our own comfort level. As you might expect, the women did most of the sharing.

One man, however, had some insightful comments that I found helpful. I'm not exactly sure what kind of a man I expected at such a meeting, but I know this man was not it. He was a plumbing supply distributor and stood well over six feet with the frame to match. I had assumed his wife drug him along to the meeting until he spoke about some of the same struggles I was going through, especially the challenge of not being able to fix what was wrong with his wife. I found myself listening intently to his words. This man had lost his son a year earlier, and he knew where I was headed on my journey. He had street credit because he was speaking from his own experience and not some abstract philosophy. I valued his opinion because he knew how bad I hurt. Later I would realize that everyone in that group understood how bad I hurt.

By the time the third meeting rolled around, Heather said I could stay home because she was comfortable going alone. Now I had a problem—my pride. I had justified the first two meetings because Heather needed the help. But going to this meeting would mean I was admitting that I needed some help too. Fortunately, by this point I had seen the immeasurable value in the group, and I set my pride aside. I *did* need help, and this group was providing it for me.

During the next two years, I only missed one meeting and often found myself looking forward to them very much. The group members shared practical advice as we all grieved, navigated holidays, and dealt with grief issues we never expected. One of those issues had to do with other people who were expecting us to grieve on their timetable. Most people would never say such a thing out loud, but if you've been on the journey of grief for very long, you can see it in their eyes when you mention a dead loved one. They may even seem exasperated that you're still talking about your loss.

If you're like I was, the idea of attending a support group may seem wrong for you. But it proved to be of such value to me that Heather and I now facilitate a group similar to the one we attended. You can find out more about groups like the one we attended by going online to www.MEND.org.

God will provide help from people in all walks of life, but those who are journeying through a similar loss have incredible insight that others often do not. I encourage you to give it a try. Asking for help in this area may be one of the best choices you make on your journey. What harm is there in setting aside your pride and taking a chance? I know support groups are not for everyone, but I also know that I was certain they could not help me, and I was wrong.

Help for Depression

At this point in my grief journey, I had made some good choices, even if mostly in spite of myself. Thank God for His protection in such things. But my situation was complicated by another loss (more about that in chapter 5), and I struggled more and more.

I felt as if I had started to recover from spiritual devastation but was now starting to fall back into it again. In hindsight, I can clearly see that I was battling with depression. I think I had a clue even then what was going on, but I didn't know what to do about it.

Heather confided in me that she was having some of the same struggles. I knew we needed more help, and I even knew what to do. I just didn't want to do it.

Finally, I made an appointment with the head of the counseling department at my graduate school. He was an instructor whom I trusted. But then I bombarded myself with doubts. *What will people think? What will they say? When this instructor sees me in class, what will he be thinking?* In spite of those nagging questions, I reminded myself that I needed to focus on dealing with my grief and taking care of Heather. We obtained the further help we needed.

In your bout with depression or perhaps another grief complication, you may recognize a need for professional help. I encourage you to act on this. As a chaplain, I commonly hear that professional counseling is too expensive. If that's your excuse, overcome that obstacle with other available resources. One of the first is likely to be your pastor. Pastoral counseling can be a wonderful help toward healing. You may think your pastor is just too busy to counsel you. Believe me, I understand the never-ending demands placed on a vocational minister. If your pastor is too busy to counsel you one-on-one, he will almost certainly recommend someone, such as an associate pastor or a local counselor who can provide services at a reduced rate.

Physicians are also often overlooked resources. I went to see mine because I was unable to sleep. I was getting one full night of sleep in an entire week, so it was a serious matter. My doctor explained that exercise and diet could play a powerful role in combating depression. He also discussed a variety of antidepressants in case those interventions weren't enough. Then he gave me some sleeping pills. I hated the idea of taking pills to sleep, but I knew I needed the help. At the same time, Heather and I began exercising together. Nothing extreme—we just went to the gym and walked on treadmills beside each other while we discussed our day. It wasn't a miracle cure, but it did help. Slowly, my thinking became clearer.

You may have a variety of reasons for wrestling with the decision to obtain professional help. I hope you will be encouraged to know that all the questions and fears I saw as barriers turned out to be my imagination. Asking for help was very hard at the time, but as I look back, I feel confident I made the right decision. God has gifted people with the ability to help others through their difficulties. Refusing help may leave you in the same condition I found myself in at the water park: treading water but going nowhere fast. Find the particular help you need for the journey, and it just might keep you from drowning.

Accepting help on your grief journey is never a sign of weakness. Search out, accept, and even ask for the help God has provided. You will look back on those whom God uses at this time in your life with sincere gratitude. Your loss will forever be connected with their help, and that is a wonderful memory.

Reflection Questions

1. What help have you refused that might actually have been helpful?
2. Who is offering to help you right now that you keep putting off?
3. Do you need to ask for help from a group or a professional?
4. What barriers keep you from asking for or accepting this help?

3

I Need Help, and I Think It's God's Fault

God is honored when you take your anger to Him.

I FELT AS IF I WERE WATCHING a scene straight out of a sad movie—the scene where the camera closes in on a group of mourners gathered around a graveside. Our pastor said a few words, and then everyone stood around feeling uncomfortable and unsure of what to do next. For a few moments the silence hung heavy, just like the breath of the mourners in the freezing air.

Family and friends extended love to Heather and me as they left to get home before the snowstorm grew worse. Eventually, I stood alone beside Caleb's grave. The cold wind numbed my face, mirroring the way I felt on the inside. I hadn't cried during the service, and I didn't cry standing there at the grave. What was wrong with me? Were all my tears gone? Maybe this was just a nightmare and I would wake up soon.

As I looked down at the tiny casket, I remember thinking, *It's a jacked-up world where they make caskets this small.* Then I felt it—a flicker of something from deep inside of me. It wasn't sorrow or sadness, but it was intense. It was a spark of anger.

Just then I was distracted from my thoughts of anger as an arm reached around my shoulder—it was my father. He had sat next to me and cried throughout the entire service, and he still had tears in his eyes. I recognized the look on his face. It was the look of a father who felt powerless to help his son. I had learned exactly what that felt like only a few days earlier. He tried to speak hope into the situation when he said, "There will be better days, son."

The words themselves sound insensitive, but as he struggled to get them out, I knew what my father meant. He was grieving the loss of a grandson, and at the same time, he was watching his own son enveloped in pain—and he could do nothing to fix it.

As we pulled away from the grave, the snow began to fall heavily. It was covering the ground and beginning to cover the road. I felt that flicker of anger again—*I can't believe I have to leave my son outside in the middle of a snowstorm.*

A New Year

Days passed quickly as the holidays came and went. My numbness remained, but the idea of a new year seemed hopeful. I had managed to complete my work from the fall semester, with some gracious extensions, and it was now time to start my spring courses.

My previous excitement of training for the ministry had vanished. Instead, I found myself just going through the motions. The debates and discussions that once captured my attention now seemed pointless and annoying.

Life back at the apartment was different as well. Have you ever walked up the stairs to your home having no idea what to expect on the other side of the door? That's how I came home from class each day. Heather was trying to organize and pay our medical bills. Policy changes throughout her hospital stay meant we had three different insurance companies to deal with. Heather told the story of what happened to our son over and over to countless insurance and hospital billing agents. Most days I opened the door to find her in tears. The anger that had once been a simple flicker was beginning to grow. I was torn apart watching my wife hurt so badly. Nothing I did seemed to help, and I became even more frustrated at our circumstances.

I turned to God and asked for help, but He seemed distant and silent. This was really apparent when we went to church. I just couldn't bring myself to sing the worship songs anymore. I looked around at the other people and thought, *They wouldn't sing like that if they knew what the world was really like. They don't have a clue.* Why did I feel anger toward total strangers? The answer finally hit me—I wasn't angry at them. I was angry at God.

Until then, I had been certain that the only way we would get through the loss of our son was with God's help. Now, my confidence in God was beginning to fade. I didn't doubt God's existence or that He was all-powerful or even that He loved me.

In fact, I was firmly convinced these things were true—and that left me confused and angry. Why didn't He do something about my situation? I had put it all on the line to serve Him in ministry, so why did He seem to be abandoning me when I needed Him the most? The flicker of anger had burst into full flame.

I was uncomfortable with my anger toward God. Do you ever wonder if God is going to strike you dead because of a particular thought? In my anger I had a lot of those thoughts, so I figured the best solution was to keep God at a distance. I know that sounds wrong, but intense anger doesn't promote clear thinking. In my frustration, I gave serious thought to quitting school. God let my son die, so why should I devote my life to serving Him? But because the spring semester was already paid for, I delayed my decision. I figured I might as well get my money's worth.

Instead of quitting school, I chose to give God the silent treatment. I stopped praying. My Bible became just another textbook.

Semper Fidelis

Tom (not his real name) was a Marine. The Marine motto *Semper Fidelis*, which means "always faithful," expresses a value Tom embraced to his core. He also was firmly convinced that God too was always faithful. This belief turned out to hold true even when Tom became angry at God.

Tom's commitment to the Marines was almost finished when the war in Iraq started. He learned that his time would be extended and that he would deploy into a difficult combat zone. Tom was proud to serve his country and did his duty faithfully. There is an old joke that there are no atheists in fox-holes. And although Tom's relationship with God didn't begin in Iraq, he certainly grew closer to God throughout the deployment. Tom attended chapel regularly, finding great support and encouragement from the chaplain. He found time to read his Bible and pray. He felt God give him strength in tangible ways as he endured the atrocities of war. He especially felt God's strength the day he provided security and watched as a mass grave was uncovered.

Tom also saw God's miraculous protection while he was at war. On one occasion, Tom was in the backseat of a High Mobility Multipurpose Wheeled Vehicle (HMMWV) that was traveling at the rear of a convoy, driving about 55 mph back to the base. Suddenly, Tom was engulfed in a roaring explosion, and then everything went black for a moment. When Tom opened his eyes, dust was everywhere. He felt the jolt of the HMMWV crashing to the ground after having been blown several feet into the air by a roadside bomb. The turret gunner was yelling, and Tom remembers his team getting on the radio as they drove out of the ambush zone. A quick check revealed only minor injuries, so they continued to the base.

Once on base, they were able to do a more thorough assessment of the damage. The turret gunner had minor cuts from flying rocks. The rest of the team members were bruised from being tossed around inside the vehicle. Amazingly, the only damage to the unarmored HMMWV was a cracked windshield.

Tom was convinced he had just been part of a miracle, but he became even more certain when he returned to the scene of the explosion. He watched as a robot discovered a second bomb that was set to explode shortly after the first one. After it was destroyed, Tom climbed into the crater left by the bomb that blew up his vehicle. It was about five feet wide and came to the top of his knees. Bomb experts explained that the bomb that hit Tom's vehicle had a kill radius of more than forty-five feet. It exploded only eight feet from the driver's side door. Tom's team should have been killed or at least severely injured. The second bomb that hadn't exploded had a kill radius of almost twice that size. Tom felt that rush known only to people experiencing or seeing a miracle firsthand. He praised God to all who would listen.

Tom continued to enjoy an amazing closeness with God throughout the remainder of the deployment, but everything changed when he returned home. He discovered that life had continued for everyone else while he was away. In some respects, he had lost the better part of a year of his life. Tom would tell you today that he should have taken time to grieve when he got home. He needed to grieve the loss of a year with friends and family and the loss of the man he used to be—war most certainly changes a man. Tom didn't understand this at the time, and he started feeling numb. His personal assessment was that he was an "emotional brick." In the numbness, God began to grow distant.

Financial pressures forced Tom to return to work before he wanted to, and anger began to flicker. Tom's emotional distance was frustrating for his wife, and their talks quickly became screaming matches. Tom's anger was blazing out of control.

Tom's intense anger continued over the next few years. He became especially disgusted with the way most people fail to appreciate life. Tom had learned firsthand how easily life can be taken away, and now he showed little patience for others who lacked that understanding. A dangerous driver risking others' lives could send him into a rage. Tom's relationship with God also continued to change—God had already seemed distant; now the distance was also clouded by anger.

In a short time, Tom's life began to fall apart. His anger eventually cost him his job. His company even took steps to ensure he was ostracized from getting a similar position elsewhere. The money he so carefully saved while in Iraq quickly disappeared. And although Tom began to focus his energy on restoring his marriage, out of nowhere, his wife announced that she wanted a divorce. It tore him apart, and the anger returned with a vengeance. How could God let him lose everything after he had served his country so well? Why wouldn't God help him save his marriage?

Tom's Return to God

Tom had hit rock bottom after losing so much. He was tired of trying to fix his problems, only to watch them grow worse. As a last resort, Tom took his anger to God. He told God that he was angry about the way his life had turned out. He expressed how much he hurt because of each of these losses and because things just weren't fair.

Tom used a journal to record his prayers and his grief journey. He can read through those pages now and see how his anger in general, and especially his anger with God, has faded. The process took some time—anger did not leave overnight, and it still returns at times. Tom continues to practice what he learned the hard way. He takes it all to God—the good, the bad, and the ugly.

Tom's hope for you is that his story will serve as a warning against cultivating and harboring anger. The anger will come, but you get to choose what you will do with it. You can keep God at a distance, or you can get alone with Him and get real. He knows what you are thinking anyway, so just be honest. The alternative is to allow that anger to become an inner bitterness that grows into a monster out of control. Once it takes control, you could lose everything. Tom wishes desperately he did not have to lose so much to learn this lesson.

My Return to God

As for me, my story picks up again as the spring semester continued, as did my anger toward God. In fact, anger in every area of my life was becoming a normal reaction. I was flat ticked off at the world and didn't care who knew it.

For an assignment for one of my courses that semester, I read several sections of the Bible. In the book of Psalms, I discovered something I had never noticed before. Many of these prayers contained a raw honesty that expressed exactly what I was feeling. "LORD, how long will You continually forget me? How long will You hide Your face from me? How long will I store up anxious concerns within me, agony in my mind every day? How long will my enemy dominate me?" (Psalm 13:1-2). I was impressed; here was a man with the nerve to rapid fire some tough questions at God. Can't you just hear the frustration and the volume growing as he cries out over and over? I felt the same way: forgotten by God, anxious, and dominated by my anger. If God included this in the Bible, I reasoned, maybe I could approach Him the same way without being struck dead. Maybe—but I wasn't quite convinced. I continued to read through the Psalms.

"My God, my God, why have You forsaken me? Why are You so far from my deliverance and from my words of groaning? My God, I cry by day, but You do not answer, by night, yet I have no rest" (Psalm 22:1-2). This man must have known intense grief, because his story sounded a lot like mine. He had plenty of questions for God, questions that were filled with pain. Yet God remained silent during the day and throughout sleepless nights.

One day as I was reading, I broke my silence with God. I had found permission to express my anger and ask my questions. *God, why did You let my son die? Why am I on the edge of financial ruin? Why can't I help Heather? Why won't You do anything when I know You can?*

God did not answer my questions, but He did listen. I never once felt that God was upset with me for questioning Him or bringing my anger to Him. Please don't misunderstand what I am saying. This wasn't just a one-time session of me blowing off steam, and then everything was all right. It took a while for my attitude of anger to fade as I continued to take it to Him. I believe God is honored when we take our anger to Him. It is an invitation of sorts—we are asking Him to join us on our grief journey.

In many other psalms, people cry out to God in pain and anger. I encourage you to find the ones that express your feelings and adopt their language. These psalms do more than simply give us permission to take our anger to God. They also show us the progression that our anger will go through. They eventually lead to hope and praise, as illustrated by one of

GRIEVE LIKE A MAN

the psalms we looked at previously. "I will sing to the LORD because He has treated me generously" (Psalm 13:6). Many of us take months or even longer to get to this point, but I found encouragement in knowing that someone so angry at God was finally able to praise Him again.

Anger Unchecked

So what happens when you refuse to take your anger to God? You may be one of those people who actually enjoy the distraction your anger provides. You would rather be mad than have to think about your loss. If that means a damaged relationship with God, then so be it. If God wanted a close relationship with you, He would have prevented your loss in the first place, right? This is common thinking when grief is complicated with anger, but it is absolutely wrong. This is illustrated powerfully in the life of Moses.

If you were to list the greatest leaders the nation of Israel has ever seen, Moses would be at the top. God gave him the responsibility to lead the Israelites out of slavery in Egypt and into a land God had set aside just for them. It was a difficult task to say the least, with many complications and disappointments along the way. But I want to focus on one particular incident in which Moses let anger rule while he was grieving. You can read the account in Numbers 20:1-13.

As the leader of a huge group of people, Moses had to deal with backbiting, gossip, power plays, and never-ending complaints. He was a target for all of it. If tabloids had existed in his day, he would have lived on the front pages. If you are in leadership, you can fully appreciate how frustrating and thankless

Moses' job must have been. He certainly was not perfect, but throughout these numerous incidents, he consistently took his frustrations to God.

Then Moses suddenly lost his sister Miriam. Their relationship hadn't always been a good one, but she was still his sister, so I believe Moses entered a tough time of grief at her death. Often public figures are denied the time and privacy needed for grief. This was certainly the case for Moses—just look at what happens next. The people he was leading surrounded him and started complaining. They even pelted him with question after question about where to get water. Imagine thousands of three-year-olds screaming, "I want a drink!" over and over, and you'll get the picture. If that doesn't make you smile, remember their accusations—they were blaming Moses because water was tough to find in the middle of a desert.

Moses had to be ticked off at this point, but he took the people's concerns to God. God tells Moses to get a special staff, gather all the complainers, and speak to a rock. God would get the glory for water coming out of the rock as He met the people's need. I wonder what Moses was thinking as he went to retrieve the staff. Was anger boiling deep inside of him? Was he thinking to himself, *I can't believe these people would treat me this way after all I've done for them! Don't they know my sister just died and that I miss her?* Moses gets the staff and screams at the group. He lets loose and gives them a piece of his mind. As his anger continues to unfold, Moses takes the staff and smacks the rock twice, causing water to gush out. In so doing, Moses disobeyed God, showed a lack of trust, and drew attention to himself. As a result, Moses is told that he will not be allowed to enter the land he was leading the people to. Moses was punished for his sin of disobedience and not for his anger. His anger did cause him to pull away from God, though, and a life lived apart from God will inevitably lead to trouble. When anger gets out of hand, and it always does when not taken to God, there is a danger of sin and serious consequences.

If you find yourself enjoying anger for a season, I encourage you to learn from Moses' mistake. Anger may feel justified and can even provide a false sense of control. That false sense of control drives many men to the point where anger in fact becomes the one in control. But if your anger controls you, you will never be proud of your actions, and grief will still be waiting patiently after the smoke clears. Make the decision right now to take that anger to God. He is big enough to handle it and guide you through it.

Reflection Questions

1. Has a distance developed between you and God after your loss?

2. What are you afraid to ask God or say to Him?

3. What emotions do the psalmists bluntly and honestly share with God?

4. How would it feel to finally be able to let go of the rage and anger?

4

Sometimes God Sends
a Basketball Team

*Other men have a part to
play in your grieving.*

I was 11 years old, and it was going to be my big day.

At three a.m. I jumped out of bed and threw on my clothes. It was the middle of November, and I put on several layers for warmth because I would be outside most of the day. As I attached a knife to my belt, I felt a surge of excitement. Knives can be dangerous, and to be trusted with one at my age made me feel like a man. My excitement grew as I carefully placed extra rifle rounds in my jacket pocket. It was the first deer season that I was allowed to carry a rifle. This was an important rite of passage in my family for boys exploring emerging manhood. I went upstairs around three-thirty and waited for my dad to wake up. He had told me to be ready at five, but like a boy waiting for Christmas morning, I knew I wouldn't fall back asleep. I passed the time by daydreaming about the record-breaking buck I would kill that year.

My big chance arrived early that afternoon. I was set up in a prime spot when a huge deer walked right in front of me. In reality it was a very small doe, but everything seems a lot bigger when your heart is pounding out of your chest. I took careful aim and pulled the trigger. The deer ran away, and I was left wondering what had happened. My dad arrived shortly after I missed the deer. I told the story carefully and showed him exactly where the deer was when I shot. He then gave me some advice on how to improve my shot. He also emphasized the importance of shooting with a safe background. I missed the deer, but the bullet had continued harmlessly into a hill behind it. He praised my safe shooting and told me that everyone misses at some point. Then he shared a story about one of his missed opportunities. I learned so many lessons that season—how to judge the size and sex of a deer simply by looking at its tracks, the importance of wind direction while hunting, and the proper way to ask a farmer for permission to hunt. I did not get a deer that first year, but I did learn skills that I still use when I hunt today.

What do you love to do in your free time? Whatever it is, there's a good chance you learned how to do it from another man. He might not have been your father—maybe a friend or mentor shared his hobby with you. If you're like me, you still enjoy sharing that hobby with other men. I still enjoy deer hunting with my brother in the fall.

Now think for a moment about your grief. Did another man teach you how to grieve? My father taught me a lot of lessons, be he never taught me how to grieve. The closest I got to learning about men's grief was through observation. My father could not even discuss the death of his mother, my grandmother. She died when I was five, and I have only a few memories of her. My brother was an infant when she died, so from time to time, he asked questions about her. I remember my father leaving the dinner table during one of these conversations to avoid crying in front of us. That taught me that men don't cry and that they don't talk about their losses. You may have been told flat out to stop crying and "be a man." These lessons are common, but they are not helpful. Fortunately, there are better lessons to be learned about grief, and other men can help us discover them.

Learning from Other Men

The idea of grieving without spending time with other men seems to be a fairly recent concept. I'm not suggesting that men used to schedule time to help each other grieve; it simply occurred naturally. In the past—and still today in many cultures—men gathered as they carried out the necessary duties associated with someone dying. This included things like cleaning the body, preparing the burial site, or even building a casket. I'm convinced that during these events, men talked and grieved together. As the young boys accompanied the older men during these events, they learned about grieving through observation and participation. Today, this type of gathering does not occur out of necessity as it did back then, but it can still be of great value.

My graduate school curriculum required groups of students

to meet over a two-year period outside of the classroom. My group consisted of five other men and their wives. We met about once a week during each semester. When Heather entered the hospital to deliver Caleb, the couples in our group were some of the only people we knew in Dallas. And because our school was just a couple of blocks from the hospital, the men made a habit of bringing their lunches to Heather's room and eating. The nurses called them Heather's basketball team because there were five of them. They and their wives were sources of support and strength throughout Heather's stay. All five were there early the next morning after Caleb died. Two of these men even made the seven-hour drive to attend his funeral.

Over the next year and a half, I grieved with these men. I say "with" because I learned that each of them also had to process the loss of Caleb. Our meetings were confidential, so I didn't have to worry about anything I said being repeated. At first I did most of the talking, and they listened. I processed my anger, my hurt, and the helplessness I felt to help Heather. These were all men training to be pastors, and each of them had traits I wanted to emulate in my own ministry. Permission to grieve from men you respect is a powerful thing, and I believe it allowed me to move forward on my grief journey. These men never judged what I said or attempted to offer easy answers, and eventually they even asked some tough questions of their own. Many of the markers you are reading about were uncovered in this group.

One of these group members became a very close friend. I continued to meet for lunch regularly with Luke even after the group work had ended. Again, he mostly listened as I spoke about struggles related to my grief. You may think our lunches sound like therapy sessions, but in reality we talked about all kinds of things. It was during regular conversation and talking about football scores that such issues would sometimes come up. I think that's what made it so beneficial—just two guys being real with each other.

Somewhere along the line, Luke presented Heather and me with a wonderful gift that remains a precious treasure to this day—a song he began working on after Caleb died. Luke is a musician, so this was one of the ways he processed his grief. He said that Caleb's death was one of the first times he could ever remember praying and caring so deeply and not getting the answer he wanted from God. Look at the lyrics written by Luke Hatfield.

Caleb

It was God's will to give him life.
Arrived eleven twelve a.m. December 1, 2003.
The doctors whisked him right away.
    "He's very sick" is all they'd say.
We've begged and prayed, both now and then,
"Your healing power, Lord, let us see."
I wonder still, "Why all this strife?"

You were lying there so still.
Departed five fifteen p.m. December 1, 2003.
Only six short, precious hours—a life and
    death with so much power.
All for naught have my prayers been?
Your will, O Father, could this be—
A heart hole never to be filled?

Why'd You send him just to die?
Don't You see the tears we've cried?
Lord, how can we understand?
Please help us, God, to trust Your plan.

I wanted you to live so bad.
And when you died I felt so mad.
But in my heart, there's hope you're glad.
Just wish you could have known your dad.

She carried you for seven months,
And only got to hold you once.
It doesn't seem like near enough,
Just wish you could have known her love.

It was Your will to live this life.
Arrived to find a humble bed, years ago—2003.
The shepherds came without delay,
And angels sang for joy that day.

You had no place to lay Your head.
Our Father's love You let us see.
But still Your years were filled with strife.

You were hanging there so still.
Departed on a cross, betrayed—abandoned,
    broken and alone.
After six horrific hours—a life and death with
    so much power.
It was our Father You obeyed,
And when 'twas finished, You took Your throne!
It's our heart's hole You died to fill.

"For you I sent Him just to die.
'Father, forgive them,' was His cry.
You'll never fully understand,
But children, you can trust My plan."

I figured at some level our meetings had to be a burden for Luke. How much fun could it possibly be to meet with a guy who talks about his dead son so much? This kind of thinking keeps many men from talking with their friends. Maybe you've told yourself this lie: Everyone has enough problems of their own, so they don't need to deal with mine. I realized just how wrong my thinking was when I read the words above. Luke's viewpoint regarding the time we met together is fascinating to me. He has told me that he actually feels privileged to have spent the time together. As I was simply being honest, we both learned a great deal. He learned about his own grief journey, how to walk with someone through tragedy, and what compassion looks like when you jump into a muddy mess to help a friend to the other side.

A Self-Made Man

Mark (not his real name) was living the American dream. His home in sunny Southern California could have easily served as the inspiration for an oil painting. The hacienda-style house was tucked between two orchards—almond trees in the front and fruit trees in the back. The lush and perfectly manicured lawn belied the dry climate and grew in stark contrast with most of the parched neighboring lawns. Parked just out of sight behind the home was one of Mark's treasures, a beautiful boat. Not just any boat, mind you, but a 26-foot Sea Ray cabin cruiser. It was the perfect transport for weekend jaunts to Catalina for fine dining and scuba diving. If a weekend found Mark at home, there was always the backyard pool or hot tub for enjoyment. These were accented by a beautiful fountain and striking landscaping.

Entering the home through the garage, you would see another treasure—a perfectly detailed convertible sports car. You didn't have to look too close to see your reflection in the red paint. It had all the options, including a throaty engine that always turned heads. The home itself was well decorated with other exotic possessions and even a few pets. In addition to all this, Mark had a wonderful family to share his success with. His wife and two daughters made this house into a home.

You may be thinking that Mark must have been a doctor or a successful lawyer with a touch of gray hair at his temples. In fact, Mark was only 32 years old and had never attended college. Mark was a self-made man with a knack for real estate. His half-million-dollar yearly income easily supported the luxurious lifestyle he enjoyed. Business trips to foreign lands and power lunches at all the hot spots completed the picture.

Mark's life seemed perfect, but there was a secret lurking just below the surface. Mark was an alcoholic, and he was self-aware enough to know it. He also knew he was powerless to stop drinking.

At three o'clock one morning, Mark stood in the middle of his orchard with a bottle of whiskey in his hand. He was screaming at God. This was strange beyond the obvious reasons because Mark did not believe in God at the time—when he was sober, he was an atheist. He looked around at all his beautiful stuff and shouted at God something like this: "God, You and I had a deal! If I worked hard and got all this crap, then I was supposed to be happy! Well, I got all the crap and I'm not happy, so You didn't live up to Your end of the bargain!" That was pretty much all Mark could remember the next day as he sat in his office, pulled another bottle out of his desk drawer, and took a sip.

Alcoholics Anonymous

Mark had known he needed to quit drinking for more than seven years at this point. Then one day he felt as if someone slapped him in the head as he interviewed a new employee. The man talked about having been an alcoholic but had now been sober for many years. Deep inside Mark knew that this was something he too wanted, and he wondered how the man did it. Pride kept him from asking the question. Instead, Mark kept trying to quit on his own. He called it mental gymnastics—convincing himself that he could control something that was clearly out of control. At one point he vowed only to drink at night, only on the weekend, or only on Wednesdays. He always managed to find excuses to violate his promises as he continued to drink throughout the day, every day. It had never occurred to him that other men could have a part to play in his journey toward sobriety and the grieving he would have to do. He had done everything else on his own, so why did this have to be any different?

The answer came one day at his beautiful home. His two daughters watched a police officer secure handcuffs behind Mark's back and put him in a patrol car. They followed in another patrol car as he was taken to jail, and then they were placed in custody of other family members. In a drunken rage, Mark had assaulted his wife. Now, at rock bottom, Mark went straight from jail to a rehabilitation facility.

Mark spent a month in treatment and began attending meetings of Alcoholics Anonymous (AA). These meetings included both men and women, but it was the men who seemed to be telling Mark's own life story. This got his attention. Mark entered his first meeting believing that he was unique and that no one else would understand where he was coming from. He remembers thinking in one meeting, *I thought I was the only one in the world who did something that stupid.* Men he barely knew were giving Mark permission to do two very powerful things—grieve his losses and accept forgiveness.

Mark would never take another drink, but his sobriety did not come easy. Alcohol had been his faithful companion for more than half of his life, and its absence left a void. One of his first challenges was to learn to think clearly again. His ability to do so returned slowly over the years. He heard about similar struggles from others in AA, and this gave him hope that he was not losing his mind. In AA, Mark was given a sponsor he could call at any time. He remembers asking his sponsor how to socialize without alcohol. Mark had to learn how to talk to people without drinking—what most people learn throughout years of interaction, he had to figure out overnight. He felt like he was playing catch-up for a lot of lost time.

Mark was left with other losses to grieve as well. As a result of economic downturns and his inability to think clearly, he lost his wealth. The business with the half-million-dollar income, the beautiful home, the boat, and the cars were all gone. Bankruptcy was bad enough, but he still owed tens of thousands of dollars in taxes. These losses were difficult, but it got even worse. As he worked the steps in the AA program, he had to recall and apologize for a lot of poor behavior—each misstep was a loss to be grieved. Can you imagine being 32 years old and learning how to socialize, deal with anxiety, and make a living all over again? It would be impossible for a man to handle alone.

Mark's sponsor and his friends at AA were there every step of the way. They told him he could get through the struggles, and then they showed him how to do it. They made sure he kept moving through his grief journey. Self-pity is a hazard that has delayed many on similar journeys. Mark says one of the most important things he learned was to take the focus off himself. He focused instead on his family; they had stood beside him through his rehabilitation. Being a father to his daughters and a husband to his wife were more important than allowing himself to be overwhelmed by the mistakes he had made.

A Higher Power

The other men in AA also taught Mark about forgiveness. Part of this process was accepting that there was a higher power in the universe. For Mark it went something like this: Others asked him if he thought he was the highest form of intelligence in the universe. Mark looked at the mess his life had become and agreed that would be unlikely. His belief in God at this point was minimal at best, but the argument did make sense to him. Although Mark's understanding of the complete forgiveness available through faith in Christ would come much later, this was the beginning of a most unlikely spiritual journey. Listen as Mark explains how it started.

> I was forced to open my mind to the probability that there is something greater than us. The idea of belief became a little easier. Still, I didn't buy into the traditional "Jesus and God" model. I have seen too many church people who are notorious hypocrites and fanatics. I wasn't about to allow my mind to be bent so badly that I'd start supporting the lifestyle of TV evangelists or drink purple Kool-Aid. So, like many of the drunks I was with, I directed my faith to something tangible. My higher power became a Yucca tree. Some gal used a teddy bear, and another fellow chose a doorknob as his higher power (I'm serious). You see, we had to find something to elevate above ourselves that would help us. Since neither Elvis nor aliens were around, we had to be inventive. I know this may sound really weird, but remember, we're talking about alcoholics going through shakes, withdrawals, and serious mind adjustments. These are not people you want flying your airplane.

As Mark's grief progressed, he put the spiritual side of things, as strange as it was, on the back burner. Little did he know, though, that more than ten years later God would bring men into his life who had another role to play in his grief journey. A series of unlikely events led Mark to befriend a pastor. Through this friendship, he felt permission to ask all his questions about God, the ones that leave many people diving for cover because they are afraid lightning will strike. Listen to what Mark learned through these conversations.

> As he went on with his explanation of Christianity, something started to come to light. I've always been a student of history. Now, this preacher was demonstrating that there was proof that Jesus actually existed; a fellow named Jesus actually walked on the earth. Suddenly, we have a historical figure. Once I accepted the historical probability, the pastor offered even more evidence proving that Jesus did some pretty amazing things. The possibility of a spiritual reality started awakening in me. I weighed logic and history, which resulted in a new spirituality.

After a long time, Mark did finally become a follower of Jesus. It is clear to him now that God put the right men into his life as he grieved. They played an important role as he wrestled with sobriety and his faith. Just think how differently things might have turned out if he had refused the help of other men and the things they had to teach him.

Find Them

Other men will serve as guides through part of your grief journey *if you will let them.* They can talk with you about the markers you're reading about in this book and help you apply them to your particular situation. At times they will challenge you, encourage you, and even warn you about the path ahead. Mark found the men who had a part to play in his grief at AA. His sponsor proved to be particularly helpful. Some of the men who helped me along my journey came into my life as part of a graduate school curriculum. I don't know where the men who have a part to play in your grief will come from, but I encourage you to find them. It may be a group or just one particular friend. Look for them and take advantage of their knowledge. Do not become discouraged with friends who are unable to play a part in your grief; the greatest help often seems to come from unlikely sources. Keep searching and ask God to put men in your life who are able and willing to help. Always have your eyes and mind open to the possibility that you can learn from other men.

Reflection Questions

1. Can you identify one man who may have a role to play in your grief journey?

2. Is there a group of men who are willing to walk beside you in this time of grief?

3. What can you do right now to find or spend time with such men?

5

Time to Man Up

*You can be a hero in just
a few simple words.*

IF YOU'RE LIKE I WAS earlier in my grief journey, the idea of being a hero amid grief probably seems ridiculous. Keep reading; it's not what you're thinking.

Six months after Caleb died, Heather and I had reached an impasse. Disagreements in a marriage can be tough enough, but add grief to the equation, and you have a recipe for disaster. Heather wanted to try to have another child; I did not. I couldn't imagine exposing myself to the possibility of more pain. We had agreed to disagree, but the topic came up for conversation more and more. A decision would have to be made, and we felt God was leading each of us in opposite directions.

Around this time Heather and I offered to watch some friends' kids so they could enjoy a date night. We, of course, were cool babysitters, so we let the kids stay up late. I carried the sleeping three-year-old to her room and tucked her into bed. As a sweet, soft voice whispered "good night," it hit me—maybe I would be missing something if we didn't have another child. I explored my reasoning over the next few days. Would it be worth the risk? I came to realize that this was an issue of control for me; I thought I could protect myself from future hurt by eliminating any risk.

You may think this applies only in the area of losing a baby, but I assure you that's not true. Loss has a way of causing men to build walls of protection, but if you build enough walls, you will eventually end up in a prison cell. This is particularly dangerous in the area of communication. Often, men do not share their grief journeys with the women in their lives because they believe talking about their sadness would cause the people they love even more pain. Men think that being a hero means internalizing hurt and thereby protecting others. They "take one for the team," as the saying goes. But in reality, this seemingly chivalrous act has destroyed many relationships.

Baby August

Heather and I did eventually make the mutual decision to try to have another baby, and it didn't take long. Within a couple of weeks, Heather was pregnant. With Caleb, it had taken a long time and many doctors' visits for Heather to become pregnant. Naturally, we were overjoyed with the ease of this second pregnancy.

The loss of Caleb meant this was immediately considered

a high-risk pregnancy, so we had a very early ultrasound. We held our breath as the technician searched for our baby with the machine. We both exhaled heavily the first time we saw the tiny heartbeat. I quietly thanked God as I held Heather's hand. After the measurements and pictures were complete, the technician said, "Everything looks good, but…" My heart sank when I heard that three-letter word. I was focused as he continued. "The sack around the baby is a little misshaped. This happens sometimes, so we'll make another appointment and check again soon." The doctor told us not to assume the worst and said we would probably know more in a couple of weeks.

I tried to stay busy for those two weeks, but worry remained a constant companion. I couldn't imagine losing another child, and I certainly didn't want to go through all that pain again.

As we arrived at that next appointment, I parked in front of the office, and we just sat in the truck for a moment. Finally, I said, "I don't think this is going to be good news." Heather nodded her head in agreement as I pulled a Bible from under the seat. I read Psalm 27, which begins, "The LORD is my light and my salvation—whom should I fear? The LORD is the stronghold of my life—of whom should I be afraid?" I wanted those words to be true for my life, but the truth is that I was afraid.

Minutes later, I stood next to the bed as the technician began his work. I know technicians are supposed to refer patients to their doctors, but it's pretty obvious what's going on when they don't point out a heartbeat. I watched the screen as hope faded with each passing second. The technician finished, told us to see our doctor, and then said what we already knew—the baby was gone. I held Heather's hand as she began to cry; our baby August had died.

In some respects we were well equipped to deal with this loss. We were already attending a support group and had many close friends willing to help. We even had one advantage that we lacked when Caleb died—we were now active in our church, which offered even more support. For a brief period of time I probably thought I had this grief thing all figured out, but I would soon learn another lesson. The miscarriage of a child, maybe more than any other loss, emphasizes just how differently men and women grieve.

He Doesn't Care

I listened as a young woman whom I'll call Annie told her story. She had recently miscarried a child—her grief was fresh and raw. Annie grew louder and more frustrated as she spoke to the group, "You know what really makes me mad! My husband doesn't even care that our baby died!" At one point this statement would have left me shocked and thinking that Annie's husband must be a first-class jerk. In actuality, I wasn't surprised in the least to hear such a comment. I had heard it many times before, and I have heard it many times since. I have listened to wives, mothers, sisters, and friends all tell me that the men in their lives don't seem to care about whatever loss they've just experienced. Although there may indeed be some men who don't care, I can assure you that's true for only a small percentage of those who are accused of it.

I had met Annie's husband, whom I'll call Josh, and I knew that her accusation was untrue. Josh was a caring husband who was sad over the loss of their baby, but he had no clue about how to help his wife. So why did Annie think he didn't care about their loss? I saw two main reasons. First, Annie had a different relationship with their child than Josh did. Annie's body had begun to experience the changes only a pregnant woman can fully know. She bonded with their child in a way that Josh simply couldn't. There hadn't been an early ultrasound, so Josh didn't get to hear or see the baby's heartbeat. Without the tangible aspects of loss, which men seem to need, Josh was left to grieve the loss of the dreams he had for this baby and his family. Even this proved somewhat difficult for Josh because he didn't know if he lost a son or a daughter. The dreams he had for each were quite different. Josh and Annie had lost the same baby, but that loss impacted each of them in unique ways. Neither of them understood this at the time, which left Annie feeling as if she were grieving alone. In this instance Josh's grief journey was progressing more quickly, but Annie interpreted this as apathy.

There was another aspect to Josh's grief that Annie didn't experience, and this was the second reason for the misunderstanding. Josh was able to see, touch, and hear his wife's hurt. Just as most husbands would, he longed to help his wife, but he felt helpless to do so. He was left grieving the loss of Annie's happiness. He couldn't say anything that would fix the situation, so Josh resolved to help his wife by not sharing his own pain. At least he could keep her from having to endure his grief. Josh thought internalizing his own pain was a sacrifice his wife would appreciate.

When you consider the anger that accompanies grief, it's easy to see how this circumstance is a disaster looking for a place to happen. It usually plays out something like this—Josh opens the door and finds Annie crying. He touches her shoulder and attempts to comfort her.

JOSH: "What's wrong, sweetheart?"

ANNIE: "What's wrong? What's wrong! How could you not know what's wrong!"

JOSH: "I know, I know."

ANNIE: "You don't know! You don't even seem to care, you never even cry! Why don't you care that our baby died?"

JOSH: "How dare you say I don't care! I'm just trying to help!"

The encounter may continue for a while, but it doesn't matter—neither of them is listening at this point. They are both hurt and offended simply because they don't understand the other person's point of view. They become outlets for each other's anger, and the screaming matches continue. The release feels good for a few minutes, but each exchange chips away at the foundation of their marriage. Josh and Annie were lucky to find the answer to this problem in time. Unfortunately, many do not discover the power of a few simple words until it is too late.

A Few More Words

Take a moment and think about the different extremes men experience when they are grieving. In one extreme, a man is completely open with his grief. This man has no problem showing emotion in public and sharing his grief journey with others. In the other extreme, a man never discusses his loss and would certainly never show emotion in front of someone else, even a close family member. Men grieve differently and fall at different points on this continuum. Take a moment and think about where you would fall.

One Scriptural example of this is the story of a man named Lazarus and Jesus' reaction to his death. If you have ever felt misunderstood in your grief, you are in good company because so was Jesus. The story is found in John 11. Mary and Martha were dear friends of Jesus, and they sent a message to Him that their brother Lazarus was deathly ill. Jesus waited two days before He began the journey to meet them. When Jesus arrived, Lazarus had already been in his tomb for four days. Mary and Martha didn't understand why Jesus waited so long before coming to them.

In fact, Mary didn't even go out with Martha to meet Jesus. I would imagine she was frustrated and angry—I sure would have been. When Mary finally did see Jesus, she made the same statement Martha made when she first saw Him: "Lord, if You had been here, my brother would not have died!" (John 11:32). She was crying at His feet at this point.

Now look at what Jesus did when He was misunderstood in His grief. He did not argue, He did not lecture, and He did not rebuke. Instead, "Jesus wept" (verse 35). He chose to share a little of His own grief with the women He loved. Remember, Jesus had known for days that Lazarus was dead. He had time to process the event before He arrived at the tomb, but He still chose to join with His friends in grief. Others who were watching misunderstood Jesus' grief too: "The Jews said, 'See how He loved him!' But some of them said, 'Couldn't He who opened the blind man's eyes also have kept this man from dying?'" (verse 36).

Some saw Jesus' tears for what they were meant to be—an expression of His grief. Others, however, thought the tears were signs of weakness. They thought Jesus was crying because He was unable heal to Lazarus. The remainder of the story proves this was not true. Jesus did raise His friend from the dead.

If Jesus was misunderstood in a moment of grief, we shouldn't be too surprised that the women in our lives may misunderstand us. But we should learn from His example. This means sharing our grief with the women in our lives at a level we can find comfortable. Communication is the key. You might be thinking, *No problem here. I'm not comfortable sharing anything!* If that's the case, the title of this chapter is for you—it's time for you to man up. This business of grieving isn't easy, and if you want to be a hero, you may very well have to extend your comfort zone. It's not easy, but isn't she worth it?

I'm definitely a man who does most of his grieving in private. I'm not comfortable showing emotion in public. I knew this tendency left Heather and me exposed to the same scenario Josh and Annie faced. We had lost so much at this point, and we had a very serious conversation about protecting our marriage. I didn't attempt to change where I was on the grief continuum. I still needed privacy for my grief. But I did share just a little of what I felt with Heather. I did this through short, simple statements. I would tell Heather, "I read through the sympathy cards again last night." That was it—no further comment needed. It let her know that I was grieving but that I didn't want to share any more.

During the most difficult days, we made a habit of doing this just before we went to sleep. Lying in the dark, we would discuss our days. She did most of the talking, but I would chime in at times. Often, I simply said, "I feel that way too." This was a process that took some time, but I resolved that

Heather would never think I didn't care about our losses. A few simple words can protect your relationships too.

There is a danger in this process that I encourage ladies to avoid. You may be tempted to push for more and more information about your man's grief. Please understand that the simple statements he's sharing may be very difficult for him. He may share more as time passes and the journey progresses, but then again, he might not. Each man has a unique personality and grieves in his own way. Some women believe that if the men in their lives were truly grieving, those men would at least cry at some point. Search your views carefully—do you believe that grief equals crying? This is simply not the case for many men, and later we will look at some of the unique ways men choose to process their grief. Even if tears are part of the equation, the crying might not happen with or in front of you.

Heather has written her story below to help men see the value in sharing their grief journeys with the women they love. It should also help the ladies as they seek to formulate their own expectations for the grieving men in their lives.

Heather's Story

When Caleb died and Jon was sitting by my hospital bed, I had no doubt that this would grieve him as well. We prayed together and prepared ourselves for our family's arrival from Missouri. When the family arrived, everyone cried with us and hugged us, but then very quickly something changed. The family focused on me instead of us as a couple. Everyone seemed to ask, "How is she?" instead of "How are you both?" Right off the bat, people projected the expectation that I was hurting more than Jon was.

Over the course of the next few months, Jon and I developed a routine to our grief. When we were alone, he would hold me and let me cry, often hiding his own tears, but I was never worried that he wasn't grieving. We would go to bed each night talking about our day, and I gained an amazing insight into his grief. I would sob and yell about something stupid someone had said to me as he held my hand in the dark. He would be angry about school or my fight with the insurance company, and I would get glimpses into his pain. I was comfortable knowing it was within his terms. In the dark, I couldn't see whether he was crying, and truth be told, it didn't matter. He was there. He was listening. He was sharing with me, albeit small amounts. Just showing up made him a hero to me, and together we got through each day.

We'd been married long enough for me to know that Jon is guarded with his emotions. I learned early in our marriage (when he was a police officer) that there are simply some things he won't be comfortable telling me. It annoyed me to an extreme, but when I tried to push for more, I got nothing!

I sometimes wonder why we women have to learn this the hard way. We are never thankful for what little we might get from the men in our lives. We constantly want to push for more details, more tears, more emotion, more…more being like us. It doesn't make any sense. We love them because they're different from us. They're strong, stable, and frankly, not driven to insanity every 28 days. Why then do we try to dismiss these differences when it comes to grief? Instead, we should embrace the differences and allow the men in our lives to share as much or as little as they need to.

I think part of our inability to allow men to grieve in their own way has to do with the images we see in pop culture. One of my favorite examples is in the movie *The Holiday* with Cameron Diaz and Jude Law. In the movie, she can't cry—she's the antithesis of most women, and we accept the ridiculousness of her character as completely fiction. He, on the other hand, is a self-proclaimed weeper, and all women fall madly in love with his character when watching the movie.

"See, he's terribly sexy and manly, and yet he can cry."

"Why can't all men be so comfortable sharing their feelings and *brave* enough to cry?"

We've all had thoughts like these, and yet in reality, they're completely false. We've concocted a fairy tale, and our inability to separate truth from fiction causes many problems in our relationships with the men in our lives.

Jon's "manning up" and participation in our grief journey together was difficult for him. He's not a weeper. I knew that and was thankful for his efforts to share with me. It gave me a comfort level to address another issue that surfaced: *Why didn't he know what I needed?*

How selfish we women become in grief. If your husband didn't know he needed to get you flowers on the anniversary of your first date, what makes you think he's automatically going to know you cried all day and simply want to be taken out to dinner? If you need that, you must tell him.

I've shared this on numerous occasions with women in our support group. Initially they respond, "But he should *know* I need this—I shouldn't have to tell him."

I usually counter with, "Before your loss, would you have known how to act or what to say?"

"No," they typically respond with their eyes turned down. "Then how could he know either?"

Grief is a learning process. It's difficult enough without forcing unrealistic expectations on our loved ones. Don't add the burden of mind reading to the men in your life. Tell them what you need and when you need it. You'll save yourself—and them—the heartache of unmet expectations.

That leads me back to nearly six months after Caleb died. We had agreed to start trying again, although Jon was somewhat reluctant. We continued our nightly discussions even as we joyfully expected our second child. Then the unthinkable happened. We lost another baby. We were devastated and angry. At least I was.

Suddenly I felt very alone. During our nightly discussions, Jon would say "I'm sorry" more often than "Yeah, I get that... I feel the same way."

Where did he go? Where was the hero I so needed? He was right there...and then he was gone! Now, I felt as if he wasn't grieving with me, but was next to me while I grieved alone. I assumed his silence was punishment for me pushing to have more children too soon. That added guilt to my grief in addition to the failure I was already feeling because my body failed my two children. It was a recipe for disaster.

What I didn't realize is that Jon would grieve August much differently than he did Caleb. I thought, *Why? They are both our babies, and now they're dead.* Again, I found myself projecting an unrealistic expectation on him. When I stepped back and logically analyzed the situation—not an easy task, mind you—I realized that I had barely gotten to know August in the short time the baby grew in my womb. How could I ever expect Jon to have the connection to August that he had with Caleb? He never felt August kick as he had Caleb. He never saw a face on an ultrasound. Granted, I didn't either, but I did experience those things that are available only to the mother early in pregnancy. I was sick. I was sore. I was up three times a night to go to the bathroom. All those things that are uniquely female—annoying and blessed in the same moment, because they meant I was a mother again. Until a father can see, feel, and experience a baby, it's unrealistic to expect him to grieve the same way.

Once again, we found ourselves on the same grief journey, but we were looking in two opposite directions. Thankfully, our experience and the support of others who had been down the same path helped us move forward. I removed the expectation that Jon would automatically know what I needed. I removed the unrealistic expectation that he would have the same connection to August that I did. I went to him and explained how I felt and what I needed. And then it happened—my hero returned. Just as a knight in shining armor can't rescue a princess unless he knows where to find her, Jon couldn't give me what I needed unless I showed him.

What did I need?

I simply needed to know that he hurt for August—not necessarily with the same intensity as he did for Caleb, but just that he hurt at all. Our marriage started with two simple words, and Jon saved it with the same two: "I do." That's all I needed to know.

Reflection Questions

1. What could you tell the woman in your life that would provide insight into your grief?

2. What is stopping you from doing so?

3. Ladies, is there something you need from the man you're grieving with that you are expecting him to automatically realize?

4. What is stopping you from telling him what you need right now?

6

I'm Going Fishing

Men process grief through action.

"WHAT WOULD YOU LIKE TO DO to celebrate Father's Day this year?" My wife's question prompted me to think about my two children. Caleb had died a year and a half before, and August had been gone for ten months. It would be my first Father's Day with two children in heaven. As I was lost in my thoughts, my wife continued, "Do you have any ideas, or would you just like me to plan something?"

I told her I would think about it and let her know. Like most men, I'm impossible to buy a gift for. If I want something, I generally go and get it myself. If I haven't already bought it, it's probably so specific that nobody else could find it for me anyway. This has prompted Heather to be very creative as she plans for special events. This year she settled on making a gourmet Italian dinner. We were still in Dallas, and the markets there offered ingredients that we had trouble finding outside the large city. The day before Father's Day, I was surprised to see a variety of unusual products in the refrigerator. I could hardly wait to see what my wife would create from it all.

Sometimes the anticipation of holidays that remind us of our loss can be more difficult than the actual day itself, but that was not the case for me this year. The day before Father's Day was a wonderful Saturday, filled with lots of joy and laughter. I even had an unusually long conversation with my mother on the phone that day. We often talked during the weekend, but I rarely spoke on the phone to anyone for more than an hour. As we finished our conversation, she asked if I wanted to talk to my dad, and I said, "No, I'll talk with him tomorrow on Father's Day when I call." As bedtime drew near, the day ended with us laughing at a silly TV show.

And then the phone rang. My heart sank as I could barely make out what my distraught mother was saying. My father had passed out, and she wanted us to pray for him. They lived way out in the country, so a neighbor was performing CPR. As I hung up the phone I sat down on the bed, stunned.

Heather entered the bedroom knowing something was wrong just from hearing my side of the phone call. I began to cry as I said, "I think Dad just died." She said a prayer as we held each other once again amid the terror of losing someone we loved. The neighbor was an EMT who had been trained by my brother, Michael. The phone rang again, and this time it was Michael on the other end. He asked if I had talked to Mom and then said, "These things usually don't turn out well."

Michael was driving to their house and expected to beat the ambulance.

It was about 11 p.m. when the phone rang again, and it was Mom. She was calm and speaking slowly as she told me what I already knew—Dad had died. I confirmed that Michael was with her and told her we were on our way.

A Long Road Home

Thanks to Heather, we were packed quickly and ready to leave. It would be about a seven-hour drive. Heather offered to drive, but I insisted. We didn't talk much, and eventually Heather drifted in and out of sleep. I tried to wrap my mind around what was going on, but it seemed impossible to think clearly. As we crossed the state line into Oklahoma I glanced at the clock, and it was after midnight. My first Father's Day without my dad. I was sad, angry, and still hoping it was all a bad dream.

Somewhere during that drive it hit me—why hadn't I talked to Dad on the phone yesterday? *God, why wouldn't You prompt me to talk to him if You knew it was going to be my last chance? How could You let this happen now when Father's Day is tough enough already? How much more loss am I going to have to take anyway!* I had long since learned the value of taking my anger to God. I glanced over to make sure Heather was asleep as tears of frustration and hurt started falling.

It was still early in the morning when we finally arrived at Michael's house. My mother was awake, so Heather and I sat with her. I called family, friends, and Mom's pastor. Michael and I remained at Mom's side through most of the next week. A lot of people came to the visitation, and as I watched friends come and go, another realization hit me. Jaime, Michael's wife, was pregnant, and my dad would never get to meet that child. My dad never met any of his grandchildren before he died. What was God thinking? Although this realization would be tough at any time, right now it seemed to be an extra slap in the face.

After a busy week with Mom, Heather and I returned to Dallas so I could complete my summer courses and she could return to work. When we got to our apartment, the refrigerator was full of spoiled delicacies—now a reminder of my losses, of so many wonderful possibilities that had all been ruined.

During the weeks that followed, I felt stuck. Whenever I thought about my dad, the same questions I had asked before came right back into my mind, and I was left frustrated. I kept asking them over and over again without finding answers. I was stuck on the trail and didn't have any idea of how to move forward on my grief journey.

I finally discovered the answer quite by accident.

I had some time off between my last summer course and the beginning of my very busy chaplain clinical training. I decided it would be a good time to return to Missouri and check on my mother. Heather was busy at work, so I went alone. I honestly thought I was simply making sure everything was going smoothly at Mom's house. Mom had been blessed with a wonderful support network that included family, friends, and her church group. These individuals took very seriously the biblical mandate to care for widows, and I thank God for each of them. Their diligent work meant that there were very few tasks that I had to do.

As I looked for something to do, I noticed that my dad's

gun collection needed some attention, so I spent the remainder of the week cleaning these guns. You may laugh at the thought of a man stuck in grief spending a week handling various firearms! I'm not suggesting that guns are part of grieving, but I do believe that men grieve through action. I just happened to discover this amid the action of cleaning a gun collection.

The first gun I cleaned was a 7mm Remington Magnum rifle. As I was removing the bolt, I remembered that the last time I killed a deer, I had used that very gun. My rifle had malfunctioned, so I borrowed it from Dad and was somewhat unfamiliar with it. When I took a shot at a deer, I was unaccustomed to its recoil, and the scope hit me in the nose. The cut left a scar that's visible to this day. My dad was watching me, and when he learned that I was all right, he laughed for what seemed like days. He loved to retell that story and laugh all over again.

As I continued cleaning, I didn't realize what was happening. For the first time since my dad's death I was able to think about him without asking unanswerable questions.

The next gun was a Remington 20 gauge shotgun. I had carried it the first time I went quail hunting with Dad and had used it to kill my very first bird. That gun was followed by a .22 caliber rifle that Dad always carried raccoon hunting. It reminded me of the night a raccoon jumped out of a tree and came six inches from landing squarely on my head.

There were enough firearms and stories to last throughout the week. In my mind I relived rites of passage that included things like being trusted to hunt alone with prized bird dogs. I laughed and cried a lot as I cleaned that collection. Just doing something helped me begin processing my grief.

A Fisherman

Pete was a lot like many of us; he enjoyed family, friends, and fishing. He also made mistakes from time to time, and one of those managed to hurt his best friend. Pete was with a group of people who were bad-mouthing his buddy, and in an effort to fit in he decided to join in.

It might have ended as just a small mistake, but his comments made it full circle back to his friend. Pete got that horrible feeling in the pit of his stomach when he learned his friend had heard everything he said. Pete knew he had to apologize, but he never got around to it.

Then one morning he awoke to news that shook him to the core; his friend had been murdered—the latest victim of gang violence in the capital city. Pete was in shock as family and friends stayed at his side for more than a week. Then he made a seemingly strange decision. Out of nowhere he decided to go night fishing with a bunch of his buddies. Some of his family thought he was trying to find a distraction, others thought he was running from his pain, and still others were afraid to let him get in a boat by himself—he seemed so depressed. Pete was left with a lot of questions, and at the top was this: *Why did I say those stupid things?*

Take just a moment and think about Pete's actions. Why do you think he decided to go night fishing? If you were one of his friends, would you have gone with him? Does your opinion change when you consider that Pete was the apostle Peter and his friend was Jesus?

Peter was one of the 12 disciples. To fully understand the depth of his sorrow during these events, we must have some background. We find it in Matthew 26:31-35, 69-75. Prior to the crucifixion of Jesus, there had been an argument. Jesus told the disciples that they would all run away from Him that very night. Peter, in front of all the other disciples, said that even if everyone else ran away, he never would. Jesus then told Peter that he would not only run away but also deny Jesus three times in the process. Peter, as if responding to a double dare, told Jesus he would die before denying Jesus even once. The account continued, and Peter did, in fact, deny Jesus three times, just as predicted. Peter wept bitterly when he realized his failure.

Shortly after these denials, Jesus was crucified. In the days that followed, Peter must have wrestled with various aspects of grief. He would have been grieving his failure, complicated by the perceived loss of his friends' respect. He also would have been grieving the death of his friend. This grief would have certainly been in transition, though. Peter saw the resurrected Jesus twice before he made the decision to go fishing. Such a roller coaster of emotions and grief would have left me feeling tired and confused. I think it's fair to say Peter was probably feeling something similar, yet look at what he does. Speaking with six of the disciples, Peter said, "I'm going fishing."

They responded, "We're coming with you." So they all went fishing—but they caught nothing.

Did you ever wonder what happened during that night of fishing? The Bible simply tells us that they didn't catch any fish and then jumps to the next morning, when they get to see Jesus again. I used to think this meant the trip was unsuccessful, but then I thought about the fishing trips I've been on. Success doesn't depend on how many fish are caught. I believe this night was very important in Peter's grieving process. Peter decided to get moving. He had been a professional fisherman before he became one of Jesus' disciples, so it's no surprise that he chose this activity.

I don't think it is a stretch to suggest that the night air and familiar work would have helped clear his head. Peter was also with some of his friends, the same men who heard him swear that he would die before denying Jesus. I wonder how Peter felt when they offered to join him on this trip. I bet it meant a lot to him to see this gesture of forgiveness. Amid the work and conversation, Peter saw that his friends didn't reject him just because he had failed. What a wonderful realization that must have been.

Where Are the Men?

I have made countless visits to homes as a hospice chaplain. As I pull up to the home, there are usually cars parked everywhere. Inside the home is a flurry of activity, often centered in the kitchen, where more food than an army could eat is being prepared. But oddly, most of the time there isn't a man in sight. Someone usually recognizes me and points me toward a group of close relatives gathered together, a group of all ladies. Often this group is sharing photos and scrapbooks centered on the life of their loved one who has just died. There is no reservation as they cry together, share feelings, and give lots of hugs. After I sit awhile, I almost always hear the same question: "Where did the men go?"

Repeatedly observing scenes like this left me wondering if processing grief through action is a characteristic common to both men and women. After all, the death of a loved one almost always leaves ladies very busy. I've interviewed and counseled many women on their grief journeys, and they tell me that action plays a somewhat different role for them. I recognize that just like men, each woman grieves in a unique and personal way—this just seems to be a common thread that many share. Many women use action as a distraction, a way to take care of others when they really don't know what else to do. If it's not a distraction, the action is usually something practical that needs to be done regardless of the loss. People still need to be fed and so on. One woman told me that all the activities were simply tasks she needed to complete so she could have some time to grieve. The activity surrounding a loss doesn't seem to be something women use to process grief, but something they complete in an effort to get to the process of grieving. They get the stuff done so they have time to grieve.

Men, on the other hand, actually use the activity to process their grief. Let's return to our scenario, and you'll see what I mean.

Someone usually answers from the other room, "I don't know where the men went, but they're probably outside messing around." I offer to go look for them, and I almost always find the same thing. The men are gathered together, engaged in some activity. I've found them working on cars, feeding livestock, repairing plumbing, or simply watching TV in the basement. During times of grief, men will even tackle projects they've put off for ages. *Men simply need the activity to process their grief.* When I find that group of men, I usually join them without interrupting the conversation. They may start out talking about the task at hand, but often they transition into stories about the person who died.

If emotion enters into the equation, it's easily masked within the fake busyness of the activity. And if a woman should show up, for reasons I don't quite understand, the conversation turns to the mundane. I can't explain why this happens—and I'm guilty of it too in my own grief—I just know that it does. A person objectively watching all this activity might think the men are simply messing around. But in reality, the men are participating in something that's very important for their grief.

Imagine then the harm caused by another scenario, which I have seen played out. A woman walks in to find her husband messing around with the guys and thinks they're insensitive and just wasting time. In an effort to promote healthy grieving, she insists that he leave that activity and join the group of ladies looking at photos. The result is that he gets angry, and his wife has circumvented the grieving process she was trying so hard to promote.

Application

Three types of activity seem to be helpful for grieving men. The first is to simply get moving. The activity may not have any specific connection to the loss, but simply doing something can be of great value. In those early days, it's almost impossible to think clearly and be creative. I stumbled into cleaning my dad's gun collection as part of my grief, but there is no need to worry about finding this type of correlation to your loss. Go take a walk and get some fresh air; exercise alone can help clear your mind. This doesn't need to be complicated. Simply do activities you enjoy. Our minds stay hazy and our grief stalls when we just sit at home and do nothing. Play a round of golf, go for a drive, take the kids to a park, build something, or shoot some rounds at your local range.

The second type of activity involves doing something with other men. We have already seen that other men have a part to play in our grieving. If you're still struggling with this, take a page out of Peter's life and have your male friends join you in some activity. Think about a modern-day fishing trip with your friends for a moment. There won't be any pressure to discuss your loss, but opportunities will almost certainly occur. If you choose to talk about it, you have the perfect setup. You don't have to look at your buddy while you are talking because your attention is expected to remain on the rod or fly.

Men seem to be more comfortable with heavier conversation when they don't have to look at someone. I think this is one of the reasons women tell me they have great talks with their husbands in the car; his attention remains on the road. Keeping your attention on a fishing rod also gives you a way out if you need it. If you become uncomfortable with your emotions, you simply stop talking. Your buddy is fine with the abrupt ending; talking might scare the fish anyway.

The third type of helpful activity involves doing something that serves as a direct reminder of your loss. If you lost a loved one, this may be an activity you always enjoyed doing with that person. Michael and I still hunt together, something we always did with our dad. If you asked either of us if this was a part of processing our grief, we would probably laugh, but it clearly serves that purpose. During these hunts we retell stories about our dad and some of the crazy things he did while hunting. Hunting season was the time of year when his attention was very focused on his sons. We do a lot of laughing and remembering.

I know a man who used to work on cars with his dad. When his dad died, his grief journey included working on cars with his dad's tools. Each of the tools told a story or provided a memory about his dad. If it seems difficult to associate an activity with your particular loss, you might find this idea helpful—I have known men who found great value and privacy in writing a letter to the one they lost. As they wrote, they were able to move past areas where thoughts alone became stuck.

Reflection Questions

1. What could you do right now that would get you off the couch and moving?
2. Whom could you call to join you?
3. What type of activity would serve as a connection to your particular loss?

7

Don't Touch My Stuff

Men need their own reminders.

I HAVE SEEN IT TURN UGLY and even tear families apart—the fight for all the "stuff."

I recall one particularly horrible situation where I was paged to a hospital room and told a family was trying to make a decision about whether or not to withdraw life support from their mother. The siblings disagreed, and they wanted a referee instead of a counselor. This argument continued to unfold for several days until some hidden motives began to surface. This group of brothers and sisters were fighting over their dying mother's possessions while standing on opposite sides of her hospital bed. It was one of the saddest displays of greed I have ever seen, and I knew that one day they would regret this behavior. They were all at her bedside when the mother's life support was removed. As their mother died, they exchanged angry glances and sarcastic gestures—all because of *stuff*!

Grief itself is tough enough. But sadly, sometimes it's compounded by situations like that above. Perhaps you were always promised a precious item that did not come to you after all. It's even possible you've found a sense of control by nursing your anger toward someone who wronged you, and now it's grown into bitterness. This bitterness now controls you so deeply that whenever you think about your loss, you head toward that familiar place of resentment. Hatred and bitterness are traps we must avoid on our grief journeys. If you find yourself stuck in them, I encourage you to decide that today is a good day to climb out of those dark holes and start moving forward again. You *can* find reminders that point you toward healing instead of hatred. Let's get creative as we explore our next marker: Men need their own reminders.

A Time to Divide

Scenarios like the one above ran through my mind as I prepared for this particular day. I was going to meet Michael at my mom's house. Mom said she was ready to divide up Dad's things. I knew this necessary step was going to be difficult for her.

I made a conscious decision that I was not going to fight over anything, regardless of how much I wanted to have it. I certainly was not anticipating any problems, but I also knew that these situations make people do stupid things, and I wanted to be proud of my behavior and not regretful later on.

Michael and I watched as Mom produced numerous items

including some we had never seen before. Mom explained what they were and where they came from, and we made our choices. The only time Michael and I disagreed was when we were trying to convince each other to take something. He would insist that I take something so a collection could remain together, and I would do the same. As we look back on it now, we can say it was a good day. My mother has commented several times over the years about how proud she was that Michael and I were so gracious to each other.

The last thing we divided up that day was my dad's gun collection—the same one I spent a week cleaning a couple of months after he died. I spoke first and handed Michael a beautiful rifle Dad had hunted with since before either of us could remember. Michael had killed his first deer with that rifle, and I knew he wanted it very much. Michael then handed me a .22 caliber rifle. I had noticed the .22 when I was cleaning the collection, and I had no idea where Dad had gotten it or why he had kept such an ugly gun. The barrel was about half covered in rust and looked as if the gun had spent the majority of its life behind the seat of a leaky farm truck. The inside of the barrel wasn't any better. It looked like someone had used the wrong ammunition and ruined the rifling. The gun was useless, and as Michael handed it to me I remember thinking sarcastically, *Thanks a lot.* Then Michael told me about the gun. It was the only gun in Dad's collection that had belonged to our grandfather, who died when I was just a few months old. Michael said that one of our uncles had recently given him a different gun that belonged to our grandfather. He felt it would be unfair for him to have both of them. I was obviously very grateful to add that ugly gun to my own collection.

Today that same gun serves as a connection to my father and my grandfather, but it always brings a question to my mind. Why didn't Dad tell me about the history of that gun? It was obviously a significant reminder of his father because it was one of the only things my dad had kept throughout the years. Further, Dad had apparently taken the time to explain the detailed history of it to my brother. The answer to this question leads us to another revelation concerning the differences between the way men and women grieve.

Memories

There is absolutely no doubt in my mind that both men and women utilize reminders as part of their grieving process. When Caleb died, Heather cherished several possessions that provided a connection with him. The obvious things included the pictures taken by the nurse, the outfit he wore when we held him, and a small lock of his hair. They also included some gifts that were given to Heather after his death. The hospital gave us a memory box after Caleb's death that included many items. One of those items was a baby ring. Heather added this ring to a necklace she wears almost daily. The ring hangs next to a cross on that necklace to serve as a reminder and also as a conversation piece. As a somewhat unusual piece of jewelry, it often prompts questions from other people and gives Heather opportunities to share about our precious son. Heather was also given a bracelet by some of her friends at the funeral. It includes Caleb's initials, and because they are different from those of anyone else in our family, she is asked from time to time whose name they represent.

Think about the difference between the way Heather uses her reminders and the way my dad used my grandfather's gun. I have rarely known Heather to leave the house without wearing at least one piece of jewelry associated with Caleb. She wants to share the story behind her reminders.

My father, on the other hand, kept his reminder carefully locked away. Dad didn't even share the story behind it with me. This seems even more unusual considering that I talked with Dad about guns all the time.

Throughout this book, we have acknowledged that every man and every woman grieve in unique and personal ways. This is certainly true in people's use of different reminders, but I think there is a somewhat consistent difference in the way men and women utilize those reminders as part of their grieving process.

Women often use them as catalysts to share about their loss, but men seem to use them more as personal reminders and may even keep them private. This has been confirmed in my thinking time and again when I ask men and women to tell me their spouse's most prized possessions. The men can usually do this quickly because they have heard their wives tell the stories behind those possessions on numerous occasions. Some of the women can do the same if their husbands have shared the stories, but I am astounded at how often they get it wrong. They may think his prized possession is the bass boat in the garage, but in actuality it's a coin his grandfather carried through World War II. So why did the wife think it was the boat? Probably because that's what he talks about all the time, and he has never even mentioned the coin.

A common argument heard in many homes also supports

this idea. Let's say a wife wants to surprise her husband, so she spends a day cleaning out the garage. In a typical garage, this effort will produce a mountain of junk that hasn't been used in years. The wife even goes the extra mile and has someone haul all that stuff away so the husband can finally park his car inside for the first time in years. The wife waits for him to pull in the drive, and then she hits the garage door opener with a huge smile on her face.

The expectation is a big hug followed by a kiss and some kind words about her being the most wonderful woman in the world. Instead the wife hears, "What have you done! Where is my…"

You might be able to complete the sentence, probably by naming some item your wife wouldn't even recall seeing or hearing about in the past several years. And when a wife mentions this, her husband responds, "Don't touch my stuff!"

The husband in this situation may not even have a clue himself as to why he's never told his wife about his "stuff." The best answer may be to go back to our discussion of communication in chapter 5. He may be uncomfortable sharing a story about his loss. Remember the other side of that conversation—you may have to at least explain that your possession is important because it belonged to so and so or it reminds you of such and such. You can share at a level you're comfortable with in order to ensure that your treasure doesn't end up at the city dump.

In recounting this, I'm not suggesting pack-rat husbands should keep everything without ever providing an explanation. I assure you that I also like a clutter-free and organized home. Some items are just not practical to keep. An example from my hospice experience may help us men avoid the two extremes—keeping everything remotely associated with their loss versus throwing it all away in an effort to avoid the hurt.

Time to Clean House

When we experience a loss, most of us have the overwhelming desire for things to go back to the way they were just a few days, weeks, or months before. I often found myself stuck thinking, *If I could only go back to the man I was before my losses.*

This type of thinking can carry over to the area of reminders or keepsakes. We sometimes believe that if we can keep all the stuff exactly the same, we will be able to get back to that same person we were before our losses. I can't imagine the hurt that the widowers I minister to must be facing. In many cases, they have been married for 50, 60, or even 70 years. They have no idea what their lives will look like without their wives in them. Some deal with this by refusing to change anything in the house. If you walked into their homes—even a year after their loss—you would still think their wives were living. The closets, bathrooms, and bedrooms all look the same.

Others go to the opposite extreme and immediately clean house. They give away everything associated with their wives and later find themselves wishing they still had a few treasured items.

We're left with the question of how to find a healthy balance for our reminders. I certainly would not attempt to set a time frame or give a specific number of items to keep, but here are some helpful ideas. I've watched numerous men deal with stuff after the death of a loved one. The ones who seemed the happiest with their decisions took time as they made their choices. The early days of grief are not the best time for clear thinking or good decision making. There is no need to conquer the entire house in just a few days. Take time to grieve as you go through items, and ask others to help you. Your goal is to keep the reminders you truly want and to make sure other reminders are given to the individuals who wish to have them.

When I chose reminders associated with the loss of my father, I initially decided to keep everything I was offered. As time passed, I discarded some of the items and kept the ones most valuable to me. This has left me with the most treasured items, but I'm not sure I would have made the same decisions in the beginning. My discussions with other men reveal a similar process—they weed out some things as time goes by. If you have a problem letting go of anything associated with your loss, I encourage you to ask yourself this question: Is this truly a reminder or just an anchor that keeps me from moving forward in my grief?

Use Your Reminders

Men use their chosen reminders in various ways. Some are displayed, some are used, and some are packed away to be looked at only on special occasions. My friend Randy has a unique application for one of his important reminders. Randy has an absolute passion for watches. He has an impressive collection and an extensive knowledge of watch histories and makers.

As you would imagine, Randy wears a lot of different watches and is happy to talk about them with anyone who will listen. Those who are fascinated by such information, like me, will often ask him about whatever watch he happens to be wearing. One day I noticed Randy wearing a watch I hadn't seen before, and I asked him if it was new. It was actually an older watch that had belonged to his father-in-law and was given to Randy after his death. He doesn't wear it as a catalyst to tell stories about his father-in-law, although that might happen on a very rare occasion. It simply serves as a personal reminder and connection to his loss.

You may remember Tom's story in chapter 3. He was the Marine who served in Iraq. He has a very unique reminder of everything he lost. It's a piece of shrapnel from the bomb that exploded next to his HMMWV. A piece of the object meant to destroy him serves as a reminder of all he endured and the miracle he experienced while at war. Somehow being able to see or hold something gives a tangible element to grief that most men find helpful.

Our friend Mark recently passed a milestone that produced a treasured reminder. He has now been sober for more than 20 years and was given a chip at AA to mark the occasion. He has navigated a difficult journey to sobriety, and that chip tangibly reminds him of everything he has been through. He showed it to me with great pride and a huge smile.

Heather's grandfather uses a fascinating collection of letters as reminders. They were written from the front lines during WWI by his dad. They give amazing insight into what that man had to endure. Reading them from a historical perspective is captivating, but reading them as personal reminders is surely even more remarkable.

I have seen other unusual reminders, including golf clubs, Bibles, coin collections, paintings, furniture, knives, rings, and even tattoos. Your reminders will be limited only by your imagination when connecting them with your loss.

Evolution of a Reminder

This marker of a reminder may have left you frustrated because for whatever reason, you don't have such an item. The answer to such a dilemma is to create your own. This is exactly what I had to do at one point in my grief. Let me show you how this came about.

I mentioned that I was in graduate school when Caleb died. At my school, there was a lounge where students gathered to eat lunch. It was also the location of the student mailboxes and several important school offices, so the building couldn't be avoided.

There was a huge mural in this building that I initially found very encouraging, especially on days when school was not going so well. Part of the mural included a student in a graduation cap and gown holding his son while his father snapped a picture. This always brought me hope because I would take a moment to imagine that day in my life, and it gave me energy to keep going.

When Caleb died, I knew I would not be holding my son when I graduated. The image that once brought me hope became a reminder of what was missing in my life. Later, of course, I learned that my father would not be taking pictures of me at graduation. Now, the mural reminded me of two horrible losses in my life. In some ways the initial excitement I had for graduation had turned to dread.

I never did learn to appreciate that mural again, but it did help me see the power of a visual reminder. I wanted something

I could look at for comfort as I associated it with the loss of my son. The answer came when it was time to order class rings. I hadn't ordered one in high school or college, so I had already decided I would like to get one when I completed graduate school.

Heather helped me choose the design, and then I made a decision that turned it into a reminder of my loss. Instead of using my birthstone, which is customary, I used Caleb's birthstone. The December stone is a deep blue that complements the silver ring well. I wear it often, and it reminds me every time I look at it that God can help me through anything, regardless of how hopeless the situation may seem. I get comments on the ring from time to time, but no one has any idea of the symbolism it includes unless I choose to tell them.

Whatever reminders you may have or choose to create, I encourage you to let them be parts of your grieving process. Reminders can bring back memories that help you move forward in your grief. Use them in a way that fits your personality and comfort level. I trust they will eventually transition from reminders of your loss to symbols of hope.

Reflection Questions

1. Do you have a reminder of your loss? If so, take just a moment to visualize or look at it.

2. How does your reminder connect to what you lost?

3. If you don't have a reminder, what could you create to serve as one?

8

Danger!

Shortcuts lead to destruction.

Hiking is one of my favorite pastimes. I recall one day when I had the opportunity to enjoy a very simple hike with Heather and two other couples who were close friends. At the beginning of this particular trail we faced a decision. If we turned to the left, we could take a shortcut, but this shortcut takes us through some bottom land that floods easily. If we went to the right, the trail was sure to be dry, but it would take longer to reach the lake and streams that I wanted to show my friends.

The decision was left up to me, but Heather reminded me that this area of Missouri was on track for a year of record rainfall. I was certain the water would have had time to recede since the last rain, so I chose the shortcut. I ignored the first warning sign as I led Heather and the two other couples along the trail. Everything went well for the first mile. The forest had that clean smell that comes only after a recent rainfall, and to top it off, the temperature was perfect. In the middle of all this beauty I was thinking to myself, *I'm sure glad I chose to come this way. We'll get to spend extra time at the lake because I took the shortcut.*

We made it through most of the bottom land, crossed a bridge, and found a sign that read, "Trail closed due to high water." I knew the lake was only a quarter of a mile away, so I hated the thought of backtracking. I thought for just a moment and then told the group that the sign had probably been left there for several days and that the water had probably gone down by now. I removed the caution rope blocking the exit from the bridge and walked ahead, followed by a somewhat skeptical group of hikers. I had ignored warning number two.

As we came around a bend, we saw a small section of the trail covered in water. Heather shot me an "I told you so" look, but I was still unconvinced. I checked out the water and found it was only a couple of inches deep, so our group traveled through it very easily. At this point I was thinking to myself, *I knew that warning sign wasn't for a seasoned hiker like me. I can't believe they would close the trail for a couple of inches of water.* Warning number three had officially been ignored.

As we made the final turn before the lake, I imagined this group begging me to guide them on some great future expedition. They had to be impressed that my instincts had proven correct despite their doubts.

We made the turn and saw the lake. It was spectacular and only 100 yards away. When I finally took my attention off the lake, I noticed another section of the trail covered in water. It was a much larger area than before, and on closer inspection, it was too deep to cross. Heather shot me the look again, and grasping for straws, I said there had to be a way around.

I tried my best, believe me, but the only way to get to the lake was with a swimsuit. My pride took a hit every time we backtracked through one of the warnings I had ignored. The group was gracious and thought the whole thing was funny. We did make it to the lake after taking the longer trail, so the hike eventually proved to be a success. Now I can even laugh at my bad decisions.

Since that day, I've shared this story with other men, and many of them respond by sharing stories in which they too ignored warnings. Why is it that so many of us men believe that warning signs are only for other people? Why is it so hard for us to resist a shortcut? I don't know the answers to these questions, but I do know that this tendency can have devastating results when it comes to grief. Shortcuts on your grief journey can lead to destruction. What follows is a series of warning signs that can help you avoid dangerous areas while grieving.

Be aware that the temptation to take a shortcut while grieving is very real. I remember one specific instance that took place while I was grieving the three major losses I have written about. I was walking down the short hallway in our apartment in Dallas when I felt an extreme pain in my side. It was sharp enough to cause me to fall to my knees. When the pain passed, I got up and sat in a chair. Nothing was wrong with me physically—my emotional pain had just manifested itself in a physical manner.

After grieving major losses for almost two years straight, I was tired of all the pain. I wanted a shortcut that would make the pain stop immediately. This is the time when shortcuts will be the most tempting—when you are exhausted and hurting, and the journey seems impossible.

The primary goal of a grief shortcut is usually to stop the pain. The result is a temporary relief from pain followed by an even more complicated pain later in the journey. I heard one man say it this way: "Grief can be delayed, but it can't be denied. It will demand attention at some point." This is also true of the pain that is associated with our grief, and unfortunately, the longer it is delayed, the more intense it often becomes.

The Beginning of Mark's Story

In chapter 4, I told Mark's story and explained how he lost everything because of his alcoholism. I emphasized the vital role other men played in his grieving. I want to revisit Mark's story and focus on the beginning of his journey with alcohol and how it began as a grief shortcut.

When Mark was still a teen, he had the same anxiety most young men deal with when they enter high school. He wanted to find friends and a way to fit in at the huge California school he attended. This search for significance led him to sports.

His athletic abilities earned him a starting spot on the football team as a freshman. He played middle linebacker and was named defensive captain. As expected, the popularity that's often associated with star athletes soon followed. Mark had found his niche, and as a result, high school was a lot of fun. He enjoyed sports so much that next he decided to try out for the wrestling team. His school had a reputation as a wrestling powerhouse, so his success on the football field meant little to the wrestling coach. But in wrestling, Mark's abilities proved to be even more successful than they had in football. He only lost one match after facing 25 of the best wrestlers the state had to offer. It was evident to everyone that he would wrestle at the collegiate level.

Mark continued to play football during his sophomore year, and he had a great season. His team would go on to win a championship. Mark captained the defense in every game except the very last one. He had suffered a severe knee injury when he was clipped in the last playoff game. The knee required surgery and did not heal as expected. The wrestling coaches became frustrated with his slow recovery and began to turn their attention elsewhere. The accolades and attention that had come with being a star athlete also began to fade. Mark's knee would eventually be repaired by more extensive surgery, but what he valued had already been lost. His athletic career was over, and he was just 16 years old.

The losses went beyond playing football and wrestling. Mark was left to grieve the loss of his identity, his popularity, his physical abilities, and many of his friends. It shouldn't be surprising that such a young man would be tempted to take a shortcut to compensate for his losses—losses that would be a lot for even a mature man to deal with.

The shortcut Mark chose to ease the pain was alcohol. It started with sneaking drinks at home and escalated from there. Mark also found a new niche in school by playing in a rock band. All of his new friends drank alcohol, and he quickly joined them. Mark's inner anger combined with his genetic predisposition toward alcoholism created a perfect storm. You've already read the rest of his story and how this decision complicated his grief in horrible ways. It was a shortcut that clearly led to destruction.

Mark was able to keep the shortcut of alcohol hidden from most people for many years. Another grief shortcut that lurks in the darkness and shadows is pornography. Much like alcohol and drugs, porn seems to offer an alternate reality—a world of enjoyment where pain is forgotten. It's also a secret and hidden world, or so many men like to think. They justify it like this: *No one will know what I watch in my home, in my hotel room, or on my computer.*

But like every other shortcut, the pain will return when the movie is over. And when it does, it will be combined with the additional problems pornography brings with it. The addiction cycle grows out of hand as you view more porn in an attempt to mask an increasingly complicated pain. Like the alcoholic convincing himself that he only needs one more drink, you tell yourself you need just one more movie, magazine, or strip club.

It doesn't take long in this cycle before you start seeing women as objects. In your distorted state of mind, you actually convince yourself this addiction is a victimless pastime. If you're headed down this road now, stop for a moment and think about just one of the victims. Men involved in pornography who are the fathers of daughters will eventually have strained relationships with their daughters. Having spent hours training their minds to objectify women, these fathers will subconsciously pull away from their own daughters when their little girls start to become women—and guess who is more than happy to fill the void of male attention? Often it is a young man whose interests may be as self-serving as the father's was when he chose the pornography shortcut that opened the door to this problem. The shortcut of pornography has left a wake of destroyed marriages and jobs and even mental-health problems.

If this warning has impacted you, I encourage you to ask for and get help—and if getting help seems impossible, read chapter 2 again. You may have found that destruction was a mouse click away, but the good news is that help is also readily available. There are numerous resources for men wrestling with a pornography addiction. Many of these resources were produced by others who can show you firsthand how to reverse course on such a horrible shortcut. They have taken the steps you need to follow to restore your life to health.

Hatred as a Shortcut

We have already talked about dealing with anger toward God, but some men actually choose to embrace bitterness as a grief shortcut. A focused hatred on someone or something keeps them from having to deal with the pain of their loss, at least for the moment.

Hate can even provide the emotional release the hurting man needs. Screaming at someone may feel good in the short term, but regret and consequences usually follow quickly. Some men say these episodes of rage are like a drug fix—they provide short-term relief from pain, but eventually they are needed more and more often. Just as a drug defines the addict, hatred begins to define the grieving man. It's easy to see how this shortcut can leave huge waves of destruction in its wake.

I've seen many members of the military wrestle with this shortcut. They somehow believe that hatred of the enemy will help them through their grief journey. It's not a coincidence that throughout history, enemies have been given demeaning names. Hating people is a little easier when we don't perceive them as fully human. This wrong focus can distract a man from grieving for a long time—in fact, some men cling to bitterness for the rest of their lives. Is that what you want your life to look like? I have attended the funerals of bitter and angry men, and I've seen pastors struggle to find something nice to say. I can assure you I don't want my funeral to be like that, and I'm sure you don't want that for yourself either.

Heather's grandmother, whom we affectionately call Mimi, told a story that provides a powerful illustration of how one man was able to move past bitterness in his grief. Mimi has somewhat of a preoccupation with my service in the Army Reserves. Almost every time I see her, she wants to know if they will be sending me anywhere soon. I tease her about asking so much, but a quick glance always reveals that she's very serious. Mimi shares her generation's profound respect for the military, and for her it is a respect born out of loss. When she was about 12 years old, her family was notified that her older brother was killed while fighting in World War II.

At that time Mimi lived on a farm in rural Mississippi, and her family was very poor. German prisoners of war (POWs) were eventually brought to that part of the country to work in the fields. Her family's farm had the only well for miles around and was the only place the POWs could get water. The family had no specific information about the details or location of her brother's death, so one of those POWs could possibly have been responsible for killing her brother. If you were Mimi's father, what would you do? Remember, we're talking about rural Mississippi in the 1940s, so his having the only well was certainly a grand opportunity for a little revenge. Thankfully, Mimi's father made the difficult choice to avoid this shortcut.

Mimi remembers watching as the POWs drank from the pump at their farm. She had to stay in the house, but she always watched through the window. She remembers feeling hatred toward the POWs and couldn't believe that her father had chosen to be kind to them. He would speak with them and even told them about his son's death. Mimi's brothers followed his example and treated the men with kindness. Eventually, through her father's example, Mimi let go of her hatred and was able to grieve. I imagine that every time the POW work detail made its way up the drive, Mimi's father had to make the choice not to hate those men. He had to look past his anger. His choice allowed him to continue on his grief journey, and it also provided a needed example for the rest of his family. What a father and what a man!

The forgiveness Mimi's father showed is astounding, but it represents a step you will have to take to avoid the shortcut of hatred. You may be tempted to blame someone who played a role in your loss. Nursing your anger toward that person can become a default. One of the reasons for this is that anger gives us a feeling of control when our losses make us feel so out of control. You may not be able to control the company's choice to eliminate your job, but you can sure choose to blame the boss, who let you go but protected his golf buddy's position. You couldn't stop your child from dying, but you can choose to never forgive the doctor who was unable to save his or her life. You can't change the car accident that redirected your life forever, but you can hate the driver of the other vehicle. This becomes even more complicated when your loss was caused by someone's intentional and calculated act. To forgive a person who took something or someone from you in such a way may seem impossible.

The journey of forgiveness, like the journey of grief, is best traveled with God by your side. It usually goes something like this. You make a choice to forgive someone, only to have feelings of bitterness return again and again. Thoughts of that person keep you up at night until you finally conclude that you must not have truly forgiven in the first place. You have a choice at this point—to give up and continue to hate the person forever or to reflect on what forgiving him or her really involves. I won't offer a quick-and-easy explanation of what the latter choice entails, but I will say that having to confront a feeling over and over is exactly what forgiveness looks like. I have had to pray and confront bitter feelings for a long time to forgive people who wronged me in relatively minor ways compared to what you may be enduring. Each time you make the choice to forgive, the benefits are worth the struggle. This decision will destroy the other person's ability to take from you something else that is very precious—your peace. This understanding of forgiveness also empowers you to forgive someone who neither wants nor seeks your forgiveness.

You may be stepping down this shortcut by directing anger and guilt at yourself. Perhaps you feel as if you're the one to blame for your loss. You likely grasp for control through the what-if game. *What if I had done something different? What if I had been there? What if I could have stopped it? What if...?* I could go on and on, but if you are wrestling with guilt, you know all too well the questions you bombard yourself with in those quiet moments. You have probably tried to forgive yourself many times, and you have undoubtedly discovered that your forgiveness falls short.

The good news is that God provides the help we need to get off this shortcut. He offers a complete life-changing forgiveness that will not fall short. Total forgiveness and full acceptance are available through faith in Christ. With that relationship secure, we can take our continued failures and shortcomings straight to God. God doesn't have the problem we discussed above. He holds no grudges; He completely forgives those who ask Him to. What would it feel like to no longer be mad at yourself, to never again feel as if you must forever punish yourself for a mistake? God can show you the answer if you will let Him.

Other Painkillers

Unfortunately, some of the dangerous shortcuts men take as they try to bypass their grief appear harmless or even beneficial. Let's take a look at some of the socially acceptable things men turn to in an effort to ease their pain. One of my personal favorites in this category is food.

Most people will not scoff when you eat large amounts after a loss, and a few will even compliment you. To make matters worse, almost everyone seems to be an enabler—people bring comfort food straight to your house by the carload. I managed to gain about 15 pounds in the month after Caleb died.

I know one soldier who returned from a yearlong deployment in a war zone and chose to ease his grief with food. In a few months he gained more than 40 pounds, and he still hasn't lost all the weight years later. The result of this poor behavior was the same for both of us—once we stopped eating, we still had to deal with the pain. We found ourselves in exactly the same place where we first started on our grief journeys, but now we were also fat. If easing pain with food is a temptation, I urge you to beware of this shortcut. Why complicate grief with the added problem of being overweight?

Busyness is another socially acceptable alternative to dealing with the pain grief brings. I'm not talking about activities that help men process their grief in this instance. Rather, I'm referring to busyness to avoid thinking about or dealing with a loss. Men can easily find distractions at work or in a project. They focus all their attention into such things only to find that the pain still remains to be dealt with in the end. This pain becomes more complicated the more it's ignored, like a bad debt that keeps growing with huge interest.

Feeling Like a Man

You may be grieving the loss of a job, your business, or a life-long dream that will never be realized. Losses like these often attack a man's identity. Although God never intended for you to find your identity in such things, you may have bought the lie that these things would bring fulfillment.

Perhaps you will never place your hope in such things again, but for the time being you are left to grieve what feels like the loss of your manhood. If you're in this situation, please take note of the next danger sign. Our culture is obsessed with sex. It's used to sell just about everything. The same lie is told to men a thousand times a day—sexual conquest makes you a man.

Some foolish men have believed this propaganda and chosen this shortcut to avoid the pain associated with their grief.

They tell themselves something like this: *If I can just prove to myself that I'm still a man, everything will be fine.* But in the end, of course, a man still has to deal with all the pain, and now he has complicated it in a horrible way, likely destroying several lives in the process.

This shortcut rarely begins with a man going out with the specific intention of having sex in order to prove his manhood. It may start with pornography or seemingly innocent flirtations.

If someone still finds you attractive, maybe you can remove all your own doubts, right? If that woman on the computer thinks you're wonderful, maybe she's right. The problem arises at the end of all of these interactions—you still question your identity as a man. If you continue to ignore the danger signs, you will likely convince yourself that taking such a relationship just a little further is justified.

But once it has gone as far as it can go, you will be even more conflicted. You weren't created to find your identity in sex. Men who have traveled this shortcut would implore you to stay on the right trail. Ignoring this warning has cost some men their wives, children, and careers as well as the respect they were so desperately trying to find.

Baby Steps

The shortcuts we've discussed so far often involve men ignoring obvious warning signs. The next mistake I want to discuss is more subtle—like a hiker taking small missteps that eventually place him far off the intended trail. I hope our discussion of this shortcut will place a flashing danger sign at that place where you may be tempted to take the first baby step off the trail.

This is a mistake some men make while believing they are actually facilitating their grieving process by dealing with the pain accompanying their loss. This occurs when a married man turns to another woman to help process the emotions surrounding his loss. This kind of sharing of deep feelings with a woman who is not your wife or a family member is out of bounds and is trouble waiting to happen.

The first misstep in this area often occurs innocently enough. A woman at work asks about your loss while you're both eating lunch in the employee lounge. You share a little about what you're going through, and the conversation moves on. As this continues over time, you find yourself sharing things about your grief journey that you haven't told your wife. Here is where justification begins to take place. Some men actually believe this is the best person to process their grief with for several reasons. First, she listens so well, and your guy buddies would just make fun of you for talking about feelings. Second, this protects your wife because she doesn't have to deal with your pain on top of her own. Finally, you can get a woman's perspective, which will inform you as you try to help your wife.

I've already dealt with the inaccuracy of the first two justifications earlier in this book. As for the last one, a woman's perspective does have some value, but this is the wrong place to get such information. If you want to understand a woman's grief in a more profound way, I encourage you to read what women going through a similar loss have written or talk with the women in a couples' support group. I learned a great deal from both sources as I sought information that might help my wife.

I have counseled with women after the men in their lives

confided their grief to other women. They always feel emotionally betrayed. In the middle of their own grief journey, they discover new situations that leave them grieving a loss of trust from the men they need the most. They want to know why their husbands would fail to walk through grief with them while at the same time asking other women to join them on their journey. Now that you see how this can deeply hurt the woman you love, I hope you will stop in your tracks if this shortcut ever seems tempting.

The ease with which many men have found themselves on this and other shortcuts emphasizes once again the role other men have to play in your grief. A good friend can serve as an extra pair of eyes as you watch for various warning signs. He may see you starting down a particular shortcut before you even realize it. He can also pull you back on the right path when you fail to heed early warnings. Many men have been pulled from a shortcut leading to destruction by caring friends.

It's Never Too Late

We've looked at some of the most common shortcuts I have seen men take as they progress through their grief journeys. The list is not exhaustive—shortcuts can be as unique as your particular loss. I hope you will take note of the warning signs when shortcuts promise to stop the pain surrounding your loss.

You may wish you had read this chapter before you journeyed a long time on a particular shortcut. If so, and if you're hearing a voice inside of you saying it's too late, don't believe a word of it.

When I led my friends down that hiking trail, I ignored

every warning that came my way until I finally had to turn back. I hope you will stop on your shortcut this very minute and seek the help that will allow you to regain the healthy trail.

Will there be consequences for taking a shortcut? The answer is yes, but to continue on the wrong path will only make those consequences more severe in the future. I've counseled with numerous men who made the decision to turn back, and they all said it was difficult to backtrack through stupid mistakes to regain the right trail. But each of them also said the healing they experienced was worth the time and effort. They were able to pull away from the muck, mire, and filth their shortcuts led them into and grieve like men.

Reflection Questions

1. What shortcut promises to ease your pain?
2. Do you find yourself on a shortcut right now?
3. What can you do today to turn back from your shortcut?
4. Who could help you backtrack to the healthy trail?

9

A New Normal

You get to choose where you will focus.

CALEB HAD BEEN GONE for more than three years, August for just less than two and a half years, and Dad for more than a year and a half. I had been taught or had discovered the markers we have explored together. These markers had helped guide me through the most difficult times of my life. I felt as if I had done the hard work and was ready for my reward. I was truly anticipating the end of my grief journey.

I had already begun to notice a transition as far as my grief was concerned. It required much less of my attention on a day-to-day basis. Occasionally, I didn't think about Caleb, August, or Dad for an entire day. At first this was a little scary, and I worried that I might be ignoring my grief or wandering onto a shortcut. As I stopped and took a careful inventory of my emotions, I discovered that everything was fine. The next logical step from my point of view would be the conclusion of it all. At this time, I had not completely grasped the concept of a new normal.

Around this same time, we learned Heather was pregnant again. Our reaction included a weird mix of indescribable joy tempered with a tinge of terror. During the days that followed this initial reaction, we had a rather unusual conversation. We debated whether or not to tell anyone about the pregnancy. With August we had been well aware of the possibility of losing a child, so we chose to keep the pregnancy to ourselves until things had progressed. We thought we would be protecting our feelings and the feelings of all those who loved us so dearly. It ended up being a grasp for control that did little good. Everyone hurt just as deeply when I had to tell them in the same breath that we were pregnant but that August had already died.

This time we decided on a different approach and told our close friends and family about the pregnancy right away. We weren't sure what the result of this pregnancy was going to be, so we wanted to rejoice in our third child for however long we might have him or her. This may not be the most helpful decision for others in our situation, but it seemed to work well for us.

As the weeks went by, that small tinge of terror certainly had a few opportunities to take control. Bleeding led us to the doctor's office more than once in those first months. I held my breath during every ultrasound or search for a heartbeat. Each time, the baby was fine, but someone always seemed to say, "…but we are going to keep an eye on this." I was so worried about losing this baby, I couldn't seem to simply rejoice in the fact that the baby was doing so well. My mind tempered my excitement in an effort to control my sorrow if the unthinkable happened once again.

We soon learned that the baby was a girl. Heather didn't want a baby shower until after our daughter was born, but a few pink and girly items managed to show up in the room we planned to use as a nursery. Meanwhile, another doctor's appointment led to bed rest for Heather. A few months on her back in bed was the next step to ensure the little girl's safety.

Heather's confinement left me with a lot of things to take care of around the house. It was a nice distraction (remember how men love to conquer tasks). Heather camped out in our walkout basement throughout this time. This left me with free rein in the kitchen and the rest of the upstairs. After a few phone calls to Heather in the basement, I even managed to program the washing machine. The laundry room was located next to the new nursery. Each time I walked past the nursery doorway, I caught a glimpse of the new baby stuff and quietly prayed that my little girl would live.

Our daughter, Madison, was finally born just a little early and spent only a few days in the NICU. Heather had to recover from surgery again, so I spent a lot of time alone with Madison in those first days. In order for Madison to leave the NICU, she had to be able to eat on her own. Coaxing Madison to eat enough wasn't easy and took a lot of patience. I had fed babies only a couple of times in my entire life, and that had been plenty for me. But this was different. I genuinely enjoyed the time we were spending together.

One day when I arrived to feed Madison, the nurse raised

the bar—Madison needed a diaper changed. Diapers were not my cup of tea, but I decided to meet the challenge. Changing a diaper may not sound like a big deal, but it gets a lot more complicated when tubes and wires are attached to your baby's arms, legs, and torso. I saw the nurse cover several smiles to avoid laughing out loud before I got the job done.

By the time Madison was ready to go home, I had participated in everything regarding her care and done so with enthusiasm. This from a man who had never held babies for more than a few minutes at a time. Something had definitely changed.

I discovered why I had changed so drastically one night when I was trying to get Madison to go to sleep. Heather wasn't home, and Madison wouldn't stop screaming. Hours passed, and I couldn't do anything to calm her down. How can a tiny baby make a grown man feel so helpless! As I rocked her for the hundredth time, I started praying—or rather, whining at God. *Why won't she go to sleep? Why can't I figure out what is wrong?* I continued for some time, certain my eardrums were about to start bleeding.

That's when God showed me something powerful. I thought to myself, *Jon, you would give everything you own to hold one of your other children for a few moments, yet here you sit complaining about taking care of your daughter.* A rebuke like that cuts to the core, and you can bet I stopped complaining. I can't say I enjoyed the remaining hours of screaming, but I can say with certainty that I noticed a change in myself. I had a different perspective because of the losses I had endured. I saw clearly that my grief journey had not come to an end, and it was not going to. It had become a part of me, and I had the choice of where to place my focus—on what I had lost or on the new normal I had gained.

Old Normal

As you look back, you may think that before your loss, everything was wonderful. If you're like most men, you may realize that you didn't fully appreciate all the blessings you were enjoying. When you look in the mirror now, a stranger seems to be staring back at you, so you start to do everything you can to become the same man you were before your loss.

This is a wrestling match every man goes through in grief. After all, the old normal is so familiar and comfortable. But pretending to be someone else requires a lot of effort, even if that someone else is just an earlier version of you. And that effort will distract you from your grief journey and can leave you stuck talking about the good ol' days.

Parts of the old normal are probably gone forever because of your loss. Those things too need to be recognized and grieved. I had to deal with the loss of my optimism as part of letting go of the old normal. Prior to my losses, I automatically deferred to an optimistic point of view on most things. After the losses, that reaction changed to a pessimistic point of view.

When I recognized the change, I wasn't able to simply return to my old positive self, and that was incredibly frustrating. If you are dealing with letting go of the old normal, I want to encourage you—there are things you will miss, but your new normal can be even better. And here is the really exciting part: *The power to make the new normal better is in your hands*. You get to choose where you will place your focus.

We've followed Mark's journey through his markers up to now. His road toward alcoholism began when he took a grief shortcut to ease the pain of losing his athletic abilities. He stayed on that shortcut for about 16 years until everything fell apart. Then he learned that other men had a significant role to play in his grief journey as he became sober. Today, Mark has learned the value of embracing his new normal. He has not had a drink in more than 20 years and lives a wonderful life. Losing everything gave him an opportunity to start over, and for him, that included a move. That move resulted in a lot of great things, but most importantly, it saved the life of one of his daughters.

Shortly after Mark's family moved across the country, one of his daughters developed a respiratory infection. In examining her, the doctor noticed some unusual growths. Mark explained that her doctors in California had examined the growths and assured him they didn't require treatment. The new doctor insisted on doing further tests, and those tests revealed that Mark's daughter had cancer. A series of surgeries and treatments followed over the next few years, and eventually she was cancer free. It's impossible to know whether the doctors in California would have discovered their mistake in time, but the health of Mark's daughter is a wonderful thing for him to focus on as he thinks about this period in his life.

Mark still lives in the same small town he moved to from California many years ago. He owns a small business, where staff meetings may be interrupted anytime by one of his three grandchildren. He has grown to accept and even embrace his new normal. He never forgets that he is still an alcoholic, though. When opportunities arise, he continues to practice the twelfth and final step of AA, which involves helping other people. I bet the individuals he has taken to AA and sponsored are incredibly grateful for his new normal as well. Mark is left with a choice each time he thinks about his past—both the good and the bad. He puts his decision this way: "Grieving was a long-term thing for me, but I am really happy with the man I have become."

The Spiritual Element

We also saw how Mark's new normal eventually included a change in his faith and how he viewed God. Most men experience this as they seek to accept the new normal—we must come to terms with God's involvement in our loss. I had already dealt with my anger toward God, but now I found myself asking why I couldn't be the same man I was before.

I wasn't mad; I was just seeking to make sense of it all. As I returned to reading my Bible, looking for answers, I came across a verse I remembered memorizing in Sunday school as a child: "We know that all things work together for the good of those who love God" (Romans 8:28).

I remember thinking this could not include things like the losses I had suffered. There is nothing good about burying a child, is there? I read the verse over and over, and it kept staring me in the face—"*all* things." It was a long time before I began to grasp what this text was saying.

Eventually, I was able to see that good did come out of my losses. I'm not saying the losses themselves were good, but I did see God take some horrible circumstances and use them for good.

Please hear me carefully—I'm not saying God caused bad

things to happen. Rather, by His grace, He used my losses to help others. What an amazing thought that God can take whatever loss you're going through and make good come from it. You may not be able to see it yet, but just wait.

I already pointed out that the loss of my first two children has made me a better father to Madison. I'm certainly not perfect, but I do value the time we spend together. I'm certain that without the experience of my losses, I would have taken a lot of this time for granted.

I was also given the privilege of watching an amazing transformation in my dad after Caleb died. Everyone who knew him noticed his new normal. The harshness that defined him before melted away, and he became a softer man. He tried to regain his tough exterior, but it never quite fit again. I don't think anyone bought the act, and it was a nice gift to see this side of my dad for the last year and a half of his life.

I'm now able to recognize many other good things that God brought out of my losses. One of the greatest was revealed as I continued to read my Bible.

"He comforts us in all our affliction, so that we may be able to comfort those who are in any kind of affliction, through the comfort we ourselves receive from God" (2 Corinthians 1:4).

This sounded like a set of marching orders. God had brought me through my losses so I could help other people as they endured similar losses. This is why the grief journey never ends—it would be a tragedy if it did so.

Once we embrace our new normal, the loss that once threatened to destroy us will now empower us to do unbelievable good for others. This is the peace Mark finds every time he takes someone to AA. It is the peace Heather and I find every time we run a support group for parents who have lost children. It is also the peace you will find when your new normal empowers you to help others on their grief journeys. Refusing to use your new normal would be a terrible waste of all your pain and hard-earned knowledge.

Change Your Focus

The best way to take advantage of your new normal is to change your focus. Men tend to focus on their losses and what they no longer have. This is normal and part of the grief journey, but eventually, we need to be able to think about good things too. Accepting your new normal doesn't mean you're happy about the loss, but it does mean you're able to see the whole picture. Let me provide a couple of examples to help explain what I mean.

Thanksgiving is a big deal for my family. My mom goes all out to make a fantastic meal for us, and she invites all our relatives, no matter how distant. When Heather and I got married, I explained that if we ever had to divide up holidays between our families, Thanksgiving would be the one my family would want.

The only time we have missed going to my mom's house for Thanksgiving was when Heather was in the hospital just before Caleb was born. As you can imagine, Thanksgiving dinner in the hospital just wasn't the same. I was talking with Heather years later about that experience, and I commented how that was probably the saddest Thanksgiving we will ever have.

She said, "I guess it's all in how you choose to look at it. Sure, we were in the hospital, but it is also the only Thanksgiving we will ever get to spend with our son." We were talking about the exact same day, but Heather had chosen to place her focus on a good memory instead of what she lost.

I was reminded recently that when we train ourselves to focus on good things, the reaction will sometimes be automatic. I was looking at pictures from a summer vacation Heather and I took with her grandparents to Yosemite. Heather was pregnant on that trip, but we didn't know it at the time. For a long time that trip served as a reminder of the miscarriage that took place a few weeks later. Now, I look at those pictures and am thankful that we got to enjoy such a beautiful place with August our unborn daughter. Yes, we later became convinced the baby Heather was carrying was a girl and we named her August. She joined us on one of the most beautiful hikes we've ever taken. Am I still sad when I think about her? Of course. But my sorrow is tempered with these memories. The new normal includes a combination of thoughts—sadness and gladness mixed together.

This type of thinking usually doesn't come easily. It often takes quite a while to adjust to the new normal. I still work to balance thoughts of my dad. The timing of his death still fails to make sense to me. I can catch myself playing with Madison and easily drift into thoughts of how much Dad would have enjoyed getting to know her. In fact, he didn't get to meet any of his grandchildren before he died. The changes we began to see in him would have been amazing to watch as he played with Madison and her three cousins. I can focus on these mysteries, or I can choose to reflect on the good things. I was able to see a different side of my dad for a year and a half. In that time, each of us said how we felt about the other. That alone is a gift I know many men would like to have from their dads, so I catch my negative thoughts and transition them to these good things. It's all a part of fully accepting my new normal.

Farm Trucks

I have long since come to the understanding that my grief is now part of the man that I am, but the weight of it can still surprise me all these years later. These surprises usually require me to make an intentional decision about my focus.

I experienced one such surprise as I went to visit a farmer whose wife had died about a year before. I jumped into his farm truck so we could go get lunch. If you've never been in a farm truck, you need to know that it's a very distinct mode of transportation with the sights, sounds, and smells to match. Farm trucks get a little beat-up from dirt roads, fields, and hauling everything under the sun. Most of them have a rifle stored somewhere, and they all have a characteristic smell— something you might pick up from a wet dog sleeping in moldy hay. They also rattle a lot, so it can be a little difficult to talk when you're on the highway. The moment I got into that truck, my mind drifted to thoughts of my father. We had spent many hours together in his farm truck.

The drive to lunch took a while, and the truck wasn't conducive for talking, so I was left to my own thoughts. I was frustrated to be thinking about Dad when I was there to help someone else. I became even more frustrated that all I thought about was what I no longer had. It went far beyond never riding in a farm truck together again. Dad was a Vietnam veteran, and he never got to see me in my Army uniform. I wonder what he (an enlisted man) would have thought about me being an officer. I can assure you the jokes would have been never ending. He had a great sense of humor, and I miss his light-hearted sarcasm. Then there was the timing of it all—how could God have let my dad die just a few hours before Father's Day? As we pulled up to the diner, I told myself I would deal with these thoughts later, and I pushed them to the back of my mind.

After a fantastic lunch, we took a different route home. The slower pace allowed for conversation as the farmer showed me some of the places that sparked memories of his wife. I saw the church they attended, places they had picnicked, and finally the home where they had lived. He told story after story that proved he was focusing on the good memories instead of what he had lost. He hurt deeply and missed her terribly, but he was accepting his new normal. It was a reminder for me that when I returned to thoughts of my dad later that day, I needed to continue to embrace the new normal. Grief is a process that often requires making that decision again and again. If it's a difficult choice for you, please find encouragement in knowing you're not alone. You won't just wake up one day magically embracing the new normal. It takes time.

Application

When Heather and I conclude one of our support groups for parents reeling from the loss of a child, we always ask a question something like this: "We never say that our kids had to die for some good thing to happen, but often we can recognize some good things that God allowed to come from our losses. Would anyone like to share such a thing before we conclude?"

I'm often surprised at the way many of these heartbroken parents are able to share something. It may be big or small, but the recognition is a step toward their new normal. Your loss may be far different from theirs, but I encourage you to take a moment and try to identify something positive that has come out of your loss. You may be very early in your grief journey, so let me encourage you to start by being grateful that you had whatever it is you lost.

You may also be frustrated with this marker. In the middle of your pain, it may sound like a fairy tale that will never come true. If this is the case, please keep this marker in mind as your journey unfolds because the first time you are able to change your focus, even in the smallest of things, will be a great day.

Reflection Questions

1. After exploring the new normal, are you sad or encouraged that your grief journey will not end?

2. How do you feel about your grief journey becoming a part of who you are?

3. With your unique loss, who might God be asking you to help or comfort?

10

A Line in the Sand

*Make a decision to act on
what you have learned.*

THE GRIEF MARKERS WE HAVE EXPLORED together offer us a wealth of knowledge. This knowledge becomes extremely powerful when we choose to apply it to our particular losses and grief journeys. Like the markers on a hiking trail, these grief markers help us get to our destination safer and quicker than we would without them. Unfortunately, many men choose to ignore markers on their grief journey just as they do on the hiking trail. I don't want you to be one of those men, so I encourage you to draw a line in the sand right now. Let it serve as a continual reminder that today you chose to move forward and never turn back.

I will never forget the day I drew my own line in the sand. It serves as a continual reminder of God's power and His unending love for me.

Two months after my dad's death I was scheduled to begin clinical training as a hospital chaplain. I knew it was going to be very challenging because I was accepted to train at the same hospital where Caleb had died. Now I had the added challenge of recently burying my dad, so I seriously considered postponing the training. After a lot of prayer and reflection, I decided to go through with it, and I'm glad I did. During this time I would conquer some serious obstacles on my grief journey.

Perhaps the greatest obstacle was dealing with all the negative things I told myself. I was reminded daily of my own losses because I dealt with death all the time. I constantly wondered if I was going to be able to help other people when I had so much baggage of my own. Was I really good enough?

Most men ask themselves this question, though they may not admit it. For me, assurance seemed to come as I helped more and more people through difficult situations. I began to feel confident, but my training was not over yet.

I'll never forget the night I was called to one of the same hospital rooms that Heather had stayed in. A family had just received news that their baby had died in the womb. As I answered their questions, I began to realize that I had a special ability to help them. My experience was empowering my ministry in a way that allowed me to help where others couldn't.

Another day I had to help a family in the same NICU where Caleb had died. Once again, I noticed the same doubts in myself, but by God's grace I was able to assist those hurting parents. I eventually began to wonder if my doubts and negative thoughts were things I would always have to deal with. They seemed like insurmountable parts of my grief journey. I would overcome them in one situation only to have them return in the next, and that was very discouraging.

Amid these challenges, I was able to do something that really helped my grief. I was able to see the nurses who had helped Heather and me while she was in the hospital. They were now some of my coworkers, and I really enjoyed saying thank you to each of them. If you have not had the opportunity to think about the individuals who have helped you in some portion of your grief journey, I encourage you to stop for a moment and do so. Take some time to thank them with phone calls, notes, or even visits.

My training eventually came to an end, but I still had not overcome those doubts about my abilities. I was still afraid my losses would hinder my ministry instead of helping it. I knew these thoughts weren't true, and I was sick of dealing with them. It made me so mad that I decided to do something about it. I contacted the chaplain in charge of the NICU and asked if there were any patients in the bed where Caleb had died. He assured me that the area was empty, so I made a visit. I found myself standing in exactly the same spot where I had been the day Caleb died. I could still see everything so clearly. Heather and I had been rushed to his bedside. He was surrounded by nurses and a doctor who were working frantically. The doctor explained that Caleb had stopped breathing for the third time, and they needed a decision from us on how to proceed. It was clear that he was not going to make it, so we told them to stop, and as they did so, everything went silent.

I'll never forget Heather's face as she looked up at me. I

have never felt so helpless in my entire life. We held our son and said goodbye. Years later, standing alone in the same spot, the smells, sounds, and sights came back as if it happened just minutes instead of years ago. I felt tears on my face and realized they weren't part of the memory. I was crying as my thoughts returned to the present and I looked at the empty bed in front of me.

And then I was surprised to find myself experience overwhelming thankfulness toward God. I was thankful for all the people He had provided to help on my grief journey and for all the lessons I had learned. I was deeply thankful that some of those lessons helped my marriage grow stronger through the grief instead of allowing it to be destroyed. I knew God had been and would continue to be my constant companion as I grieved. I found myself having a private worship service in a most unlikely place.

As time passed at that bedside, my attention shifted to those negative thoughts and doubts I was wrestling with. I began to see them for what they were—attacks designed to stall my own grief journey and prevent me from helping other people. The thoughts were clearly lies, and I believe the father of lies, Satan, was the one on the attack. This led me to do something very unlike me—I quietly said a few words to Satan, something like these: *This is the very spot where you tried to destroy me. It almost worked; I was close to abandoning my calling out of anger. I thought all the pain and losses were just too much to handle. God had other plans, and by His power and for His glory I'm still here helping others. You failed!*

As I prayed, I no longer felt helpless. In fact, I felt the power of the Holy Spirit in an amazing way. This moment of prayer was my line in the sand—I refused to believe those lies any longer. This didn't mean I would never again face bad days and challenges as I continued on my grief journey, but it did mean I was moving forward in spite of those bad days and those challenges. Even now, that day and that prayer continue to serve as a reminder of God's power to get me through whatever difficulties may be ahead. My last experience in that NICU, like the first, changed me. I walked out a different man.

Jesus and Soda

My friend Jacob's (not his real name) story shows how the lines each of us must draw are often unique to our own situations. Jacob was doing a pretty good job of living the American dream, or so most people thought. He was an extremely skilled craftsman. His skills allowed him to demand a premium price for his time, and employers were happy to pay it. He found himself turning away work simply because there were only so many hours in a day. This success allowed him to purchase a nice home that he shared with his girlfriend. Jacob had earned great respect in his profession and his family life. He did not feel, however, that he had the respect of his girlfriend, so he worked harder in an attempt to earn it.

One evening, while up against an important deadline, Jacob was offered some methamphetamines to keep him awake so that he could finish the job. He had already been awake for 18 hours, so he decided to give it a shot just that one time to get the work done. It didn't take long before Jacob began using meth as an escape from the grief he felt because his girlfriend didn't respect him. What started as an "upper" to finish a job turned rapidly into a grief shortcut. Jacob even saw his meth purchases as acts of financial rebellion against his girlfriend. His convoluted thinking went something like this: *If she doesn't respect what I do for her, then I will just snort all the money away. See how she likes that!*

Jacob's grief shortcut led straight to the same place they all eventually do—to destruction. He was able to remain a functioning addict for many years, though, as he continued to work and demand a premium price. The money, of course, was quickly used for meth, and as any addict will tell you, there were never enough drugs.

Jacob slowly drained his significant savings to buy more and more. As the spiral continued downward, the savings dried up, and so did the quality of his work. Eventually Jacob was broke and unemployed, but he still needed the meth. He started stealing, and this continued for some time until he chose to steal from a neighbor. Jacob actually walked from his front door over to his neighbor's house in the snow, stole some items, and walked back again. Police officers simply followed his tracks straight to his house. He was arrested and put in jail.

Jacob's girlfriend had long since left their home, but she did come and bail him out of jail. As he frantically searched all his hiding spots for meth, she realized he had a serious problem. She took him to his parents for help. Jacob agreed to go, but his motives were certainly mixed at this point. He didn't want to stop using meth; he just wanted to learn to control his use better so that he could stay out of trouble. He also wanted to stay out of prison, and this was a very real fear. The incident with his neighbor was the last straw in a series of criminal activity. He hoped his parents would get him a lawyer.

When Jacob entered a rehabilitation facility that night, he wasn't drawing a line in the sand with his grief or addiction; he was simply hoping to get out of trouble. He still thought he could control his meth use at any time. He convinced himself that he was in trouble not because he was using meth, but simply because he got sloppy.

Jacob followed the rules at rehab but was really biding his time until he could return to using meth. He heard about a Bible study offered at a local church for the folks in the program. Jacob was excited to attend because they served a particular brand of soda he didn't have access to at the facility. He could have cared less about studying the Bible.

The speaker at the Bible study, an associate pastor at the church, spoke openly about his own drug addiction and road to recovery. Jacob didn't realize it at that point, but this man would play a significant role in his grief journey. The talk resonated with Jacob because it described the same self-destructive path and series of justifications he had traveled through. The pastor explained how he learned to place his hope in something other than finding a better batch of meth and getting a better high. This hit Jacob like a ton of bricks because he spent most of his time dreaming about better meth. He was convinced that if he could find a batch that wasn't mixed with so much filler, he would get the high he always wanted. This guy knew what he was talking about when it came to drugs, so Jacob thought he might know a few other things as well.

Jacob asked for a Bible that night and tried to read it when he returned to the facility. His mind was too fuzzy, so he wasn't able to make heads or tails of what he read. He did, however, decide to return to the Bible study, and when he did, soda was not his main concern. He listened as the pastor spoke once again about his past addiction. The pastor said that he was finally able to place his hope in something beyond the next fix and something beyond himself. He had found his hope in a personal relationship with Jesus Christ. This was all stuff Jacob had heard before. He knew all the slang and would have even told you he was a Christian, but this pastor's words left him realizing that something was missing.

As his mind grew clearer, Jacob eventually drew the most important line in the sand for his grief journey. He simply and quietly placed his trust in Christ. There were no magic words— just a man asking forgiveness from the Savior, who was offering it freely.

You may be wondering if Jacob's new faith solved all his problems. The answer is *absolutely not!* Sobriety was a challenge for him as he completed the program. There were also some pretty serious legal consequences to face.

I was curious how he would react when a judge refused to accept a plea bargain arranged with the prosecutors that would keep him out of jail. I got my answer the day I sat on one side of the protective glass waiting to visit him. He entered the small area on the other side smiling from ear to ear. He told me he had hope regardless of the circumstances. He had been sober for almost a year and a half when I made that visit. When his "shock time" was over, he faced a long probation and thousands of dollars of restitution payments. Jacob once again chose to focus on his freedom and his grief journey.

The grief shortcut that Jacob traveled so far down was a very difficult one to return from. I don't need to ask him if it was worth it, though. The answer is obvious when I look at his life.

Shortly after his release, he started studying to be a pastor so he could help others recover from addiction. As of this writing, he is just about to complete the college program. He is also experiencing the joys of being long removed from that toxic relationship of long ago. After Jacob actively engaged in his grief over loss of respect, loss of possessions, and a lot of bad behavior, he was able to enjoy a healthy relationship. In fact, I had the privilege of standing as a groomsman in his wedding just a short time ago. I tease him constantly that he married "up"; he always gives that ear-to-ear smile and agrees by saying, "Isn't God so good!"

Other Lines

Perhaps you remember the other unique lines drawn by men throughout this book. Tom, the Marine, drew his line in the sand when he decided to take his anger to God and once again when he went to see a counselor. My friend Luke wrote a song to move forward in his grief. Mark's line in the sand led him to return to his grief after 16 years on a shortcut and find sobriety. Jesus provided the challenging example of sharing our grief journeys with the women in our lives. The apostle Peter drew his line the day he decided to get moving and went fishing with his friends. The decisions were all different, but the results were all the same. They all faced the obstacles in their paths, and in those defining moments, they chose to grieve like men.

And Now It's Your Turn

What about you? Is it time for you to draw a line in the sand? You've seen the markers, so now it's time to make the decision to act on what you've learned. Choose to make today the day you will remember as a turning point in your grief journey.

This may mean making the choice to begin or return to a journey you have avoided for many years. Will it be painful? Yes. But it will also be worth it.

You must start moving forward. Will you do it perfectly? No, and believe me, I know how frustrating this can be for perfectionists. Grief is dynamic, personal, and unique. Just about the time you are sure you have it all figured out, it can throw you a curveball. When difficulties arise, always remember that no one has to travel through grief alone. God will be your constant trail guide if you will invite Him along for the journey. My prayer for you is that one day your loss will empower you to help others far beyond your wildest imagination.

Reflection Questions

1. Whom do you need to thank as you draw your line in the sand?

2. What line can you draw right now that will help you move forward no matter what?

3. Where do you stand when it comes to the ultimate line in the sand—what to do with Jesus?

11

Trail Guides

*Use this road map to help
others during their grief journeys.*

HAVE YOU EVER RECEIVED A CALL OR E-MAIL with distressing
news from someone you care deeply about? If you have, you
were probably stunned at first by the news of the person's loss,
but soon you likely began to wonder how in the world you
could help the person. Should you give him a call or respect
his privacy? Maybe an e-mail would work...but who knows
when he will feel like checking that again. Would a visit be the
right thing?

And once you decide how to make contact, what will you
say? You will certainly offer to help, but that's the same offer
he will likely hear from numerous people in the next few days.

How can you assure him that your offer is genuine and that you really desire to join him on his grief journey?

These are difficult questions that keep many people afraid of helping their loved ones. It's easy to become paralyzed and simply do nothing because we have no idea what we could do to help. Even if we've gone through similar losses, fear can still keep us silent. We also know that grief is unique for each individual, so how do we approach our particular loved ones who are hurting? I can't give you all the answers—hurting people and their situations are far too complicated—but I can offer some insight to help you overcome the fears that keep way too many trail guides from walking with others on their journeys.

If you wrestle with these questions, please know you're not alone and you're absolutely normal. Even the 12 disciples struggled with how to help Jesus on one of His grief journeys. You can read about it in Matthew 14.

This passage begins by describing the details surrounding the death of John the Baptist. John had been put in prison because he had the nerve to tell Herod that it was wrong for him to have taken his brother's wife, Herodias. Herod would have simply killed John on the spot, but he was afraid of the political backlash, and he was also somewhat fascinated by John. In fact, Herod was so intrigued by John, Herod would later think that Jesus was John returning from the dead!

During Herod's birthday party, his staff brought in a dancing girl who just happened to be Herodias' daughter. Then, much like a modern-day drunk making promises to a stripper, Herod makes an outlandish offer. He so enjoyed her dancing that he actually promised Herodias' daughter whatever she desired. Herodias told her daughter to ask for the head of John the Baptist on a platter. Herod seems to have quickly discovered the danger of lust-provoked promises, but he kept his word and had John beheaded.

Some of John's friends buried his body and then delivered the news to Jesus. Imagine learning that your ministry partner and beloved cousin—the man who baptized you and announced your ministry—was dead because a leader was enchanted by a stripper. Herod killed John merely to save face in front of his buddies. I would be hurting and enraged at such a wasteful injustice. Jesus suffered an extremely difficult and seemingly senseless loss.

Notice Jesus' response when He receives the news. "When Jesus heard about it, He withdrew from there by boat to a remote place to be alone" (verse 13). We know Jesus understood John's death from a divine perspective, but even He wanted some privacy for His grief. The disciples initially had something they could do to help Jesus. He wanted some privacy, and the only way to get Him away from the crowd was over the water. I bet it felt good to have something specific to do to help their grieving friend, even if it was simply rowing a boat. I think we all long to help others in their sorrow. Specific tasks empower us to do so in a concrete way.

Have you ever been sitting with a hurting friend who asked for something to eat? Everyone jumps, and ten people hit the kitchen while five more call for takeout. Perhaps this is because many people are uncomfortable with just being with a grieving person, and any request provides an opportunity to actually *do* something.

When the boat reached land, the disciples quickly discovered this was not going to be a very private place. The crowd

GRIEVE LIKE A MAN

had found an overland route and was waiting for Jesus when He stepped on the shore. Jesus had some time to think during the boat ride, but further reflection would have to wait until He could get the privacy He needed. So Jesus spent time with the crowd, but when it began to get late, the disciples encouraged Him to send the crowd away so the people could get something to eat.

Perhaps the disciples were also aware that Jesus was hurting and that this would be a good excuse to stop His work for the day. This might have been in their minds as they objected to Jesus' directive to feed the people themselves. I know we pick on the disciples for getting so focused on the here and now that they forget Jesus was in the business of doing miracles, but I think it's fair to say that they cared about their friend's grief. I certainly have anxiety when I'm trying to help someone and the circumstances seem to make my efforts impossible.

Jesus miraculously feeds the 5000 men as well as the women and children. Then He sends the disciples back across the water in the boats and dismisses the crowd. If I had been one of the disciples, I would probably feel as if I had really blown it with Jesus. *I was just trying to help Jesus get some privacy, but I messed up that whole feeding the crowd thing. Jesus ended up having to take care of it Himself instead of privately grieving over John. It wasn't bad enough that the crowd was a burden—I had to add to that burden by being thickheaded. Jesus didn't even take the time to discuss His miracle with us. He usually debriefs us, so He must be pretty angry. I can't believe how stupid I was.*

Have you ever felt like this as a trail guide? Have you ever tried to help someone only to feel as if everything you do only makes matters worse? I certainly have, and I'll bet that if you haven't experienced this yet, you will. Don't be discouraged—grief is messy. When you choose to come alongside someone who is hurting and whose thinking is clouded by grief, things get complicated.

The exciting part is that even in the mess, you can show a willingness to be there, and usually your friend will need you again soon. Avoid the temptation to bow out at this point because you are afraid of blowing it again. Notice the way Jesus returns to the disciples in this passage.

With the disciples in the boat and the crowd on their way home, Jesus finally found the privacy He was initially looking for. I bet Jesus was exhausted and faced the temptation of postponing His grief for a later time. "After dismissing the crowds, He went up on the mountain by Himself to pray. When evening came, He was there alone" (verse 23).

Jesus spent time that night in prayer with the One who would never misunderstand His grief journey. Jesus invited the perfect trail guide to join His grief journey. Later He would also return to the disciples and continue His journey with them.

Around three the next morning, Jesus returned to the disciples by walking on the water. They thought He was a ghost and were terrified. "Immediately Jesus spoke to them. 'Have courage! It is I. Don't be afraid'" (verse 27).

Jesus was clearly addressing the terror they were feeling at the thought of a ghost, but I think these comforting words went even deeper. Jesus invited Peter to join Him on the water, saved Peter from sinking, and finally entered the boat and calmed the storm. His actions showed them that even though they weren't the perfect trail guides on His grief journey, He still loved them and valued their relationships. As you consider specific ways to help your grieving friends and loved ones, you must always keep this idea in mind. You will not have all the words, and you will make mistakes. This doesn't mean you're a poor trail guide. Rather, it simply means you showed up for the journey.

Just Show Up

I began this book by helping men to recognize that grief is never convenient. Grasping this idea can help men make good choices early in their grief. The best choices focus on people. Simply being with others will help a hurting man get a good start on his grief journey.

This same principle applies to helping someone who is grieving. Rarely is grief convenient for trail guides either. You must be intentional and make the time to help. If possible, go and see your grieving loved one at the first opportunity. In some cases, the first opportunity will be minutes after the phone call alerting you to his loss. If you can't possibly show up in person, make the phone call. I have found that the call can be tougher because the grieving person can't see your expression or feel your touch. My recommendation is to use the most personal contact available. The first step to being a good trail guide often involves resisting the urge to use less personal communication, such as a text or e-mail.

After you have made the tough choice to show up, then what? We saw earlier that doing something specific to help the hurting person is often productive, but what happens when your friend doesn't need anything done? The answer is to simply be with him. Don't try to explain or give answers. Just being with a hurting person is one of the most productive things you will ever do as a trail guide. It's also one of the most difficult for most men. Remember, we have that urge to fix problems and find solutions, so the idea of simply being with someone is often uncomfortable. Freedom comes when you recognize that you can't fix the hurt and that your friend understands this.

I'm prone to try to fix situations with my words, so over the years I've learned to say something like this when I first come alongside a grieving friend or loved one: "All I can say is that I'm so sorry. I love you, and I'm here for you." After saying this or something similar, I sit down and shut my mouth. Hurting men often simply need someone to listen, and this means avoiding the temptation to respond. Let them say whatever they want to, even if it is nothing at all. Your greatest service may be sitting and supporting in silence. Or it may be sitting and supporting as your friend screams and rages. Unless you need to keep him from harm, try to remember that a little raging may be just what he needs. Will it make you uncomfortable? Probably, but remember, it's not about you at this point.

In chapter 9, you read that a man's grief journey never really ends. Yours won't end, and neither will your friend's. Instead, it will eventually become a part of who he is. So what should you do as his journey continues? Just continue to be there. Initial support is usually offered by many, but continued support remains the realm of a select few. I encourage you to be one of those few.

As the journey continues, you'll be able to use the grief markers you have learned about to help, always remembering that everyone's grief is unique. As a trail guide, you may suggest and even warn, but remember, it's never your job to push

GRIEVE LIKE A MAN

someone down the trail. Every trail has distinct obstacles, but it also has its own unique beauty and inspiration. You can choose to be a part of that for someone you love.

Thank You

If you have been a trail guide or if you are considering becoming one, thank you. It's a challenging role that involves sacrifice and courage. It's also a rewarding and fulfilling one. I learned many of the markers in this book from trail guides who joined me on my journey. There are far too many to acknowledge by name, but much like the losses they helped me grieve, each of them has now become a part of me.

156

About the Author

JONATHAN FANN is a writer and has served as a chaplain for a hospital and a hospice as well as a combat support hospital as a member of the United States Army Reserves. He is a graduate of Dallas Theological Seminary, where he earned master of arts degrees in biblical studies and Christian education.

Jonathan has been married to his wife, Heather, for more than 14 years. They have three children. Caleb and August are both in heaven, and Madison is an active three-year-old. They live in Southwest Missouri, where they codirect a support group for individuals enduring infant loss. Information about this nationwide group can be found at www.MEND.org. More information on Jonathan's speaking ministry can also be found at www.jonathanfann.com

Other fine reading from
Harvest House Publishers...

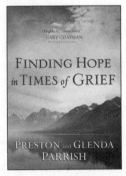

PRESTON AND GLENDA PARRISH experienced the sudden death of their 25-year-old son, Nathan, the same week that Preston's father died. In *Finding Hope in Times of Grief,* the Parrishes candidly share their story and the struggles they faced, as well as how they found hope in Christ and in the pages of the Bible. Writing from personal experience, the Parrishes come alongside others who grieve, pointing them to God's all-sufficient grace—grace that is great enough to infuse even their worst moments with His comfort. This book will help those who grieve to...

- know God's presence and peace in the midst of their suffering

- realize that hope still exists and can be known

- understand that their suffering can assume a place of purpose in their lives and in the lives of others

Finding Hope in Times of Grief points us to the surpassing hope we have in Christ and the comfort that comes ultimately from God Himself. This book will also help family members and friends better understand how to support those who grieve.

THROUGH GREAT PERSONAL LOSS, authors Cecil Murphey and Liz Allison have gained insight to share with others who are facing uncertainty, depression, and loneliness after losing a loved one. They also offer advice for those comforting someone who is grieving.

Comforting paintings by artist Michal Sparks complement brief stories, personal experiences, and prayers that offer a meaningful path toward healing for readers when they…

- feel alone and lost in their grief and want to reconnect with others and to life
- seek to make sense of their loss alongside their sense of faith, purpose, and God
- want to honor their loved one without clinging to the past in unhealthy ways

Readers are given gentle permission to grapple with doubt, seek peace, and reflect on their loss in their own way without judgment and with understanding and hope. A perfect gift for a loved one dealing with loss.